GREAT EVANGELICAL
PREACHERS OF YESTERDAY

JAMES McGRAW

GREAT EVANGELICAL
PREACHERS OF YESTERDAY

ABINGDON PRESS

NEW YORK • NASHVILLE

GREAT EVANGELICAL PREACHERS OF YESTERDAY

Copyright © 1961 by Abingdon Press

Library of Congress Catalog Card Number: 61-11785

Some of the chapters in this book
are based on articles written for
The Preacher's Magazine, published
by the Nazarene Publishing House.

SET UP, PRINTED, AND BOUND BY THE
PARTHENON   PRESS,   AT   NASHVILLE,
TENNESSEE, UNITED STATES OF AMERICA

TO MY STUDENTS

More than they know, their eager minds and searching questions have been an inspiration to their teacher

PREFACE

Exactly what it is that makes preaching great is a matter of opinion, and the diversity of opinions on this subject is what makes the study of homiletics interesting. One may wish to judge the greatness of a sermon by its effect upon those who heard it, by its content of truth as accepted by those of orthodoxy, by its qualities of "communication" with the audience, by its loyalty to church doctrines and usages, or merely by how well the preacher performed as he delivered it. Here we are interested most in the greatness of preachers based on how well they succeeded in preaching the Bible as the inspired word and in exalting Christ as the son of God.

Historically, the term "evangelical preaching" came to be associated with the protest against the formalism of Anglicanism. It laid stress upon justification by faith, which is accompanied by regeneration. It carried out the ideals of the Reformation, which in fact are the ideals of the New Testament. The strength of the Reformation was to a great degree the strength of preaching, and it was the kind of preaching which has in our times become known as evangelical preaching.

The term "evangelical" means "preaching the good news." The word has come to be associated with those who have placed greater emphasis upon the *kerygma*, "preaching the gospel," than upon that form of preaching termed *didache*, "teaching truths of God to believers." In this respect evangelical preaching is much like evangelistic preaching, yet the latter as it has become known has not always been evangelical.

Evangelical preaching traditionally has been notable as having been based on the Bible as the written revelation of God's holy will. It recognizes the inspiration of the Scriptures without necessarily accepting the views of the literalists. It is biblical preaching in the tradition of what was recently expressed by Donald G. Miller: "Unless our message is an unfolding of the meaning of the Scriptures, we are orators and not preachers. And the world will never be saved by oratory." It is preaching which resists the temptation to be diluted with too much of the preacher's personality, taking into account the truth of Principal Denney's assertion, "No man can at the same time call attention to himself and to Christ." It sends men away from the house of God not saying, "what a lovely sermon" or "what an eloquent preacher," but "what a great God!"

Such preaching as was done by the subjects studied in this book was not bound by form or method, but was guided by need. It was done for a purpose—the exaltation of Christ and the nurture of faith in his power to save. Such preaching was after the fashion of that which Phillips Brooks had in mind when he urged the students at Yale to "think no sermon good which does not do its work." "Let the end for which you preach," he said, "play freely in and modify the form of your preaching." The purpose of evangelical preaching always has been to interpret the meaning of the Bible as it reveals God's will and meets human needs. G. Campbell Morgan, an excellent example, expressed this when he declared, "Nothing can happen today to which the truth of God has not something to say."

Lyman Beecher said many times that a sermon should have one, and only one, "burning point." In evangelical preaching, that point is the fulfillment of the commission given by our Lord to Paul: "To open their eyes, and to turn them from darkness to light, and from the power of Satan unto God, that they may receive forgiveness of sins, and inheritance among them which are sanctified by faith."

Does this imply that all other preachers than those who consider themselves "evangelicals" do not have such a pur-

8

pose, do not preach Christ, do not use Bible texts? Certainly
no such implication is intended. But the significant fact is
that there is a difference in emphasis. It may be argued that
the difference is largely in the minds of those who call themselves evangelical, but the difference cannot be written off so
casually. At least fifty per cent of preachers in Christendom
today, according to one estimate, consider themselves to be
evangelical. According to the definition used here, however,
the number would be less than this, but the final decision as
to who is and who is not an evangelical will be left to those
better qualified to judge.

The decision as to which preachers should be included in
this book was not an easy one. The author anticipates criticism at this point, because of the differences of opinion
regarding what makes a preacher great and what makes him
an evangelical. As it resolved itself, it was a rather simple
solution. Those men whose preaching methods seemed to be
of greatest interest and of most value in inspiring young
ministers to preach better were the ones selected for study
in this book.

Wycliffe and Huss seemed to be good subjects with which
to begin. They represent the preaching which awakened
interest and focused attention upon truths Luther and the
others were able to portray during Reformation times.
Luther, Zwingli, and Melanchthon are seen together to help
point up the differences between German and Swiss preaching during the Reformation. Surely no book of this kind
could be complete without including John Knox, the "Thundering Scot," whose political courage and influence matched
his dedication to his God, and John Calvin's place is un-
disputed.

John Wesley is a central figure in evangelical preaching,
for it was as a result of his own "warmed heart" that he
demonstrated the significant change that can take place in
a man's preaching when "the gospel of good news" is proclaimed by a spirit-filled messenger. Those associated with
him, "the Methodists," are grouped together as would be

expected. Charles Simeon, little known but vastly important, takes his place with them.

The book includes a study of some nineteenth-century Americans and some of Britain's finest examples of evangelical preachers in the nineteenth century. One may wish others could have been included among them, but no one will wish any such names as Robertson, Maclaren, Spurgeon, Meyer, Morgan, and Jowett to be omitted.

Grateful acknowledgment is made to the publishers and authors who have made available the sources of information from which these brief bits have been gleaned, to the students whose eager curiosity and inquiring minds have been an inspiration for further study of these preachers, and to all those who have been interested enough in searching for clues toward better preaching that they may read the book. May they be rewarded with a few new ideas, some interesting moments, a fresh awareness and sensitivity toward some of the qualities which make for good preaching, and a degree of satisfaction in having lived again with these men whose stature placed them among the great evangelical preachers of yesterday.

JAMES McGRAW

CONTENTS

215 68

CHAPTER 1

John Wycliffe

1320(?)-84

Few preachers have been able with their pulpit power to influence the course of history more than did John Wycliffe, "father of the English Bible," and "morning star of the Reformation."

Born in Hipswell, near Richmond, Yorkshire, he proved himself a superior student in the elementary grades, and in later years at Oxford. At thirty-five he won his junior degree in philosophy and theology, and later became master of Balliol. The knowledge of men, the mastery of youth, the education of office, the confirming influences of responsibility, and the passion of biblical truth prepared him during these days of service as an educator for his coming influence as a reformer.

From his earliest school days Wycliffe was an intensive reader, and he developed a keen interest in the Bible. His closely read Bible made him a mighty man with the Scriptures, and it led him to the realization of perhaps his greatest contribution to history.

Wycliffe's efforts to put the Latin Vulgate translation of the Bible into the English language were not realized until a few brief years before his death, but they occupied his spare time and utmost energy until the task was completed. He is the father of the modern translators, in the opinion of many. His version in the vulgar tongue, although somewhat Latinized, is literal, plain, and "easily understood of the common people." It is the foundation of several subsequent versions, and Tyndale, in his translation, used it largely.

Two factors doubtless contributed to his compelling desire to produce a translation of the Scriptures in his native tongue. One of these was his love for the Bible and his thorough schooling in its knowledge. The other was his frequent habit of walking in the country, entering the farmhouses of the poor, where he was heartily welcomed, and of reading to the people from the Scriptures in their own tongue. He became a master of the common speech of the common folk. His love for these people, together with his love for the Bible, brought about a translation of the Scriptures in their language.

Wycliffe's trained mind and great soul soon brought him into sharp controversy with the ecclesiastical powers of the day. J. S. MacIntosh, saintly old British biographer of Reformation characters, said of John Wycliffe that his entire life was war. This war, of course, was war with the Roman church.

His zealous arguments against clerical abuses won him the support of the political anticlerical party headed by John of Gaunt. Those, by the way, who wail today that the clergy should "stay out of politics" should read their history books once again, for they will find the examples of courageous opponents of prevailing evils in Reformation times more than worthy of our emulation. Men like Luther, Huss, Zwingli, and Wycliffe did not hesitate to come to grips with the enemy.

John Wycliffe's principle of making the words of the Scripture the foundation for Christian doctrine was later one of the basic planks in the Reformation platform. Christ was dear to him, and he came to possess a unique love for the word of Christ. God's truth and God's grace were his grandest themes. As a student of Aquinas and Augustine, he was deeply pained by the political Romanism of his day. His chief theme was the grace of God as the source of salvation.

Many preachers have been noted for their excellence in one phase or the other—biblical preaching or practical appeal. Wycliffe was both biblical and practical in his approach. The underlying reason for this fact was doubtless his love for the common people coupled with his love for God's word.

No preacher ever regarded the condition of the people more sincerely or set about to help them more persistently

14

than did John Wycliffe. Mingling among them, he developed an understanding for the poor. In a day when the monks and friars were neglecting the ministry to the poor, Wycliffe's attitude was one of a shepherd rather than a hireling. Like Jesus in Galilee, John Wycliffe preached to the poor and lost the favor of those in high places. He saw ignorance as a curse to the people. He opposed their blind worship of something they did not understand while their priests made their understanding darker and their ignorance greater.

Wycliffe's purpose was to bring to the common people the truth that their way of salvation lay through intellectual and spiritual light. He sought in his preaching to quicken them by the Holy Scriptures into a knowledge of the sublime purpose of Jesus Christ and to give them an understanding of the Christian life and how it could be lived. To the peasants, John Wycliffe's message was one of hope, deliverance, and salvation in the midst of poverty, corruption, and misery.

In answer to the question, "How must the word of God be preached?" Wycliffe once answered, "Appropriately, simply, directly, and from a devout, sincere heart."

This brief statement tells a great deal about his own style in preaching. Wycliffe was not a spectacular preacher, and there is no evidence that he was an acrobat in the pulpit. He gained the attention of his hearers by his simple, straightforward appeal, by clarity of voice, by grip of logic, by simplicity of thought, and by lovable personality. He did not need a call upon outward assistance in the form of bodily gestures or wordy eloquence. He possessed a courage of convictions, a keen intellect, and a quiet but powerful consciousness of strength of character.

Someone has described his appearance in the pulpit as "tall and thin, with a long black gown, his head adorned with a full-flowing beard, exhibiting features clean and sharply cut." Leckler said of him that his eyes were clear and penetrating and his lips firm in token of firm resolution. We can be certain that his bearing was one of dignity and character.

Wycliffe was a dialectician. Few men in Christian history have equaled him in the ability to distinguish truth from error, and few could have mastered him in the debate which it seemed his lot to perform. His logical disputations brought the crowds to hear him wherever he preached and placed the pope and the priests on the defensive.

He was didactic in his method of presenting the truth; that is, he believed teaching to be an important part of preaching. He believed that expounding the word of God would bring the desired results in the hearts of men. He saw no need for "varnish" or "soft soap," but had supreme faith in the plain, unanswerable truth of the Scriptures.

Each sermon shows evidence of careful preparation. Wycliffe the scholar, the educator, the university master, had a hand in the preparation of the sermons of Wycliffe the Reformation preacher of a mighty gospel. He was at his best in debate with the ecclesiastics over the issues before the church and the people. The monks wrote lampoons; Wycliffe replied in tracts that stung like scorpions. The monks put to work their coarsest libelers and whispering campaigns. Wycliffe made all England laugh with his keen humor and dry wit. They pointed to Rome's law; he pointed to the Magna Charta and the acts of Parliament. They quoted canon law; Wycliffe replied with God's law. They called on the pope as authority; he confronted them with the authority of Christ. They appealed to the great councils; Wycliffe, to the Christian conscience and the day of judgment.

Some three hundred of Wycliffe's sermons now in print give us an insight into his method of sermon development. His sermons are vigorous in attack, clever in appeal, and eloquent in form. They are chiefly textual and expository, quite systematic in development, and unusually logical in thought succession.

In general, the sermons of John Wycliffe were founded

upon the Gospel, the Epistle, or the lesson for the day. As an expository preacher he followed scriptural divisions and expounded the truths one step at a time.

His sermon on "Charity," from I Cor. 13, begins with a contextual introduction. Wycliffe said:

Paul telleth in this chapter how men should know charity, and how men should keep charity; and this love is needful to each member of the church. First, Paul telleth how needful is charity before other things; and he begins at the highest work that man hath in holy church. . . . Afterwards, Paul saith, that if he hath prophecy, and know all secret, and have all manner of science, and if he hath belief, so much as to remove hills, and have not charity, he is nought to holy church. . . . The third, saith God in Paul, if a man deal all his goods into meats for the poor, and give his body so that he burn, as some men do for heresy, and he have not charity, it profiteth him nought to bliss.[1]

Illustrations in Wycliffe's sermons were drawn from the Scriptures, and from science, mathematics, physics, and chemistry—in which subjects he excelled as a youth at Oxford. His conclusions, in general, were résumes of his messages with a brief application and appeal. The conclusion in his sermon on "Charity," in which he lists sixteen conditions by which men may know they possess God's love in their hearts, reads: "Look thou at these conditions, whether thou have them all in thee: and if thou have them not, bestir thyself to have them whole. And then without a doubt thou hast this love that must bring thee to bliss. And of this Paul teacheth the excellency of charity." [2]

Sick, frail, and ready to die, John Wycliffe continued preaching until his second stroke. On December 31, 1384, the brave old warrior fell at the altar as he neared the part-prayer of the service in his hallowed church, and they carried him gently to his rectory, where his beloved books, his oaken table, and his Bible waited. Three days later he died.

[1] *Writings of John Wycliffe* (London: Religious Tract Society n.d.), p. 197.
[2] *Ibid.*, p. 200.

Thirty-one years after his death, at the Council of Constance, Rome sought revenge for the smarting defeats it had suffered at his hand. Tried and condemned, he was sentenced to be disinterred from his grave and his body burned. For thirteen years the order was disregarded, then finally executed. His body was burned and the ashes scattered into a brook named the Swift River near Lutterworth.

Thus his burned body symbolized the fires of love he kindled in the hearts of the poor; his ashes, "conveyed by the brook to Avon, Avon to Severn, Severn into the narrow seas, and then into the broader ocean," symbolized the doctrine of free salvation by faith, which is now dispersed all over the world.

CHAPTER 2

John Huss
1369(?)-1415

Martin Luther wrote: "When I was at Erfurt I found in the library of the convent a volume of the sermons of John Huss. On reading, I was overwhelmed with astonishment. I could not understand for what cause they had burnt so great a man, who explained the Scriptures with so much gravity and skill." [1]

The man to whom Luther paid this tribute was born of peasant Bohemian parents in July of 1369, and chose his own surname from the town of his birth, Husinetz. The earliest reliable information concerning his life dates to his scholarship in the University of Prague, where he received the degree of bachelor of free arts in 1393, and within the following three years the degrees of bachelor of theology and master of arts. He later taught at the university, became the dean of its philosophical faculty, and achieved fame as its much loved rector and spiritual leader.

John Huss is remembered as a witness and a martyr. The word martyr is used today to mean "one who dies for a cause," but it formerly meant "a witness." It gained its present meaning when many early Christians "testified" to their convictions by dying for them. In the ministry of John Huss, the Bohemian, we have an excellent example of Christian witness and Christian martyrdom.

Huss drew upon himself the disfavor of Rome when he, like Luther, spoke out against the things he found to be at variance with the teachings of the Nazarene. He was in bitter conflict with his Archbishop over the papal schism, an issue in ecclesiastical politics in his time. His opposition to the hierarchy became even more intense over the sale of indulgences, which he declared to be economic exploitation of the people and indefensible on the part of the church. He

---

[1] Herbert B. Workman, *The Dawn of Reformation* (London: The Epworth Press, 1933), II, The Age of Huss, p. 1.

saw that the claims of universal power on the part of the papacy were contradictory to the statement of Christ, "My kingdom is not of this world." As would be expected in view of the usual pattern of such things, Huss was banned from all the churches in Prague except two and was later exiled.

It was during his trial and exile that his preaching and writing achieved a peak of effectiveness. During this period of his life he attacked the religious and doctrinal foundations of the abuses and corruptions of the church. Emulation of some of the distinguishing characteristics of his pulpit power, it is hoped, will help today's evangelical preacher to stem the tide of secularism and bring Christ's way to the attention of humanity.

Huss spoke with "unction," which W. E. Sangster said is the most important quality of preaching—a quality which is observed immediately by the spiritually sensitive, and even by the insensitive who see that the preacher has "stepped aside" so that the hearers can see God. When Huss preached the people were moved. His glowing zeal for the glory of God impressed those who heard him preach. Warmth of personality and piety of spirit breathed through his words.

Huss had the fortunate and desirable quality of orderly and systematic thinking habits, and this contributed significantly to the success of his ministry. While many people of his day seemed to be content with superficiality, Huss went to the roots of things, attacking doctrinal bases for corruptions rather than the mere outward manifestions. He was thorough in whatever he undertook, and he undertook whatever he thought would please God and advance his kingdom.

His study habits during his formal education, and his desire for knowledge and understanding, which received its fulfillment during his days as a brilliant student in Prague, continued to characterize his attitudes as he developed his ministry. His intellectual power was recognized by all who heard him, even as it impressed Martin Luther when he read his sermons more than a century later. While distinguished scholars attended his church in large numbers and were thrilled by his preaching, the common people also looked upon him as their champion and defender. Peasants and royalty alike were to be found among his listeners. Is there anything that could be said of his preaching that could be more significant than this, in describing its effectiveness and its influence?

John Huss was bold to proclaim his faith and unafraid to defend it. Papal bulls did not intimidate him. Threats and abuses did not turn him from his steadfast position, and storms of ecclesiastical criticism did not veer him away from his purpose. He knew how to be tactful, yet he never vacillated when under pressure. To read some of his sermons is to feel the effect of skillful appeal, tactful suggestion, and stimulating demand.

During the increasing tensions that surrounded him in those last days of his fruitful ministry, he declared boldly:

I avow it to be my purpose to defend the truth of the Holy Scriptures, even to death, since I know that the truth stands and is forever mighty and abides eternally; and with Him there is no respecter of persons. And if the fear of death should terrify me, still I hope in my God and in the assistance of the Holy Spirit that the Lord will give me firmness. *And if I have found favor in his sight he will crown me with martyrdom.*[2] (Italics mine.)

The brand of boldness Huss had was the kind that expected opposition, welcomed it, and accepted the suffering and death that were possible by-products of it. A preacher like John Huss would apparently not be unduly impressed by negative votes, by defiant deacons, by critical "Christians," nor by bullying board members.

John Huss was dramatic in his use of illustrations but he was not an entertainer. His popularity in Prague would not have developed through sensational appeals nor superficial sentimentality. The people came in great numbers to listen

[2] Robert F. Sample, *Beacon Lights of the Reformation* (Philadelphia: Presbyterian Board of Publication and Sabbath School Work, 1880), pp. 111-12.

to the preaching of this man because his preaching was Christ-centered and biblical.

One writer, studying the life and ministry of Huss, observed that in some thirty-five letters Huss wrote there were 172 references to Scriptures. He discovered that eighteen books in the New Testament and ten in the Old Testament were quoted, and that there were 149 quotations from the New Testament and twenty-three from the Old Testament.

Preaching that is saturated with scripture and sound in biblical doctrine will have tremendous effect upon those who hear it, especially when presented by a man whose heart is burning with love for Christ, whose mind is trained and active in straight thinking and adequate knowledge, and whose life is above reproach and beyond blame.

Those who like the popular and indeed valid saying "I would rather see a sermon than hear one" or "What you are speaks so loudly I cannot hear what you are saying" would esteem the preaching of John Huss. He spoke the truth, and he put his words into actions.

Faced with the choice of recanting or burning, he stood before the Council of Constance with all the strength that remained in his body, weakened from imprisonment and disease, yet refusing to recant or change his position.

The council ordered the executioner to burn him, branded him an arch heretic, and devoted his soul to the devils in hell.

He faced eastward as they tied him to the stake, but they turned him westward, thinking it improper for a heretic to die facing the east.

While the flames leaped about his body, John Huss cried, "O Christ, Thou Son of the Living God, have mercy upon us!" Someone watching was heard to say, "What this man hath done before, we know not; but now we hear him put up excellent prayers to God." [3]

Some men are gifted at saying words that sound great,

[3] Oscar Kuhns, *John Huss: The Witness* (Cincinnati: Jennings and Graham, 1926), p. 136.

and others cannot seem to express themselves in words, and yet demonstrate with their actions that they have found the truth. John Huss died with the flames smothering the last bit of life from his body, and in so dying he put into actions the words he had so eloquently spoken: "I am glad to wear this crown of infamy, for the love of Him who has worn one of thorns." [4]

[4] *Ibid.*

CHAPTER 3

Martin Luther

1483-1546

> "Here I stand: I cannot do other-
> wise. God help me!"

These historic words were Martin Luther's answer, spoken to the papal powers gathered in the Diet of Worms in 1521, which was called to silence criticism of the Roman church and nullify his preaching of the doctrine of the forgiveness of sin. The stocky little monk gave notice in that meeting, to the listening world and to heaven and earth, that he had no intention of retracting his firm stand. A thunderbolt had struck, a light was shining in the midst of ecclesiastical and religious darkness, and the Reformation was begun.

It is not easy to characterize such a man as Martin Luther in one point of view or in a few words. He was a man of contradictions, for both the good and the bad in him were on a grand scale. His extreme violence was matched with his beautiful tenderness. His frequent coarseness— which must not be represented as being in the nature of vice —was matched by an almost surprising delicacy. His masterfulness and impatience were balanced by tact and prudence. No man of his time more powerfully broke through the barriers of artificiality to reality, and yet he never completely overcame a tendency toward superstition. His amazing self-confident egotism in his assertions before men was matched only by his utterly humble reliance upon God in his prayers. He was, indeed, a personality of great contradictions.

Luther was born of humble parents in Eisleben, Germany, in 1483. His family life was often one of struggle against want. His ancestors were sturdy, hard-working, honest peasant people; hence his physical heritage was one which cultivated in his personality the elements of strength of character, power of will, and firmness of purpose.

Luther received strict religious training in early child-

hood. His parents, pious Hans and Margarethe Luther, desired that their children be brought up in the fear of the
Lord. Since the popular religion of those days was one of
fear rather than of joy and happiness, it is no wonder that
Luther turned pale and began to tremble when as a child he
heard the name of Christ mentioned. He was taught to look
upon him as a stern and wrathful judge.

The religious training he received, together with the firmness and sometimes harshness of his father's discipline
made Martin Luther a timid boy. This was further intensified by his schooling, which in those days was anything but
a delightful episode. With many a blow of hand and rod the
schoolmaster hammered into the young minds of Martin and
his other pupils the Decalogue, the Lord's Prayer, the
Apostles' Creed, the elements of reading and writing, and
the rudiments of Latin grammar. Luther later wrote that
in the course of one single morning in that school he was
beaten no less than fifteen times.

In spite of the poverty of his family and the harshness
of scholastic discipline, Martin Luther had an excellent
education. He finished his schooling at Magdeburg and
Eisenach and was sent to the University of Erfurt, because,
as he put it, he "doubted himself." He was the most rigorous
of monks, but his monastic life became a prolonged soul
agony which was not ended until he received his light on
"justification by faith." He came to the knowledge, through
God's wonderful grace, that his salvation did not consist in
his presenting to God a credit balance in his moral life, but
was a free gift in Christ. God, here and now, was ready to
forgive any man who came to him through Christ in repentance and faith—this he came to know as he studied the
Pauline epistles and earnestly searched his soul in prayer.

The preaching of Martin Luther came into full bloom
after his experience of evangelical liberation. He preached
and lectured with a positive note born of his own assurance
of salvation by faith, but he was no less a Catholic and had
no intention of leaving the church. It was while he was a
professor at Wittenberg that the crisis in his life came. It

came about as a result of the appearance in Juterbog—near Wittenberg—of John Tetzel, preaching indulgences for the Teutonic Order. It was then that Luther posted his ninety-five theses, the event rightly reckoned as the beginning of the Reformation.

At Wittenberg Luther preached to large crowds who were eager to hear him. His fame spread over all Germany. On one occasion, when he arrived for his preaching appointment the whole population was in the fields harvesting, but they left their work and crowded into the church to hear Martin Luther. When he preached at Zwickau, speaking from a window in the city hall, 25,000 people crowded into the market place to hear him.

Almost all Luther's sermons were expository messages. He liked to preach on entire books of the Bible, two of his favorite books being Genesis and I Peter. He was fully persuaded that the chief aim of preaching was to acquaint the congregation with the great truths of the Bible, and more especially to proclaim Christ as Redeemer and Saviour.

It is interesting to note that most of his sermons which are now published were not actually written by him, but were taken down as he preached them by interested hearers. He seldom took time to revise the manuscripts. He did, however, do some sermon writing, primarily for the purpose of having them read in the churches by pastors who were too ignorant to compose their own sermons. He thought it better for all concerned that a weak preacher should read the sermon of another, rather than pass off upon his hearers one of his own poor productions!

Luther did not write out his entire sermon, as a rule, in preparation for preaching. It is remarkable that he was able to keep sight on the central thought of his text without doing so, and he told his friends on several occasions how disgusted he became with himself if he departed from what he had mentally outlined for himself in a sermon.

Luther's concept and ideal of preaching can be seen in the advice he gave to preachers:

A good preacher should have these properties and virtues: *first,* to teach systematically; *secondly,* he should have a ready wit; *thirdly,* he should be eloquent; *fourthly,* he should have a good voice; *fifthly,* a good memory; *sixthly,* he should know when to stop preaching; *seventhly,* he should be sure of his doctrine; *eighthly,* he should venture and engage body and blood, wealth, and honor in serving the Word; *ninthly,* he should suffer himself to be mocked and jeered by everyone.[1]

John Louis Nuelson quoted Luther as instructing his preachers:

A good sermon must be delivered slowly and without screaming or startling gestures. . . . Above all, a sermon must not be long. A preacher must cultivate the art of saying much in a few words. If you can not preach an hour, preach half an hour or fifteen minutes. A good preacher will stop when people are anxious to hear more of him and think the best is still coming.[2]

A sample of Luther's sense of humor is observed in his story of a good old divine who, in a hospital where his audience consisted of poor, old women, preached on the marital state, its divine sanction, and its blessings. "He is a foolish preacher who does not know how to adapt himself to his audience and to the occasion," Luther declared.

Plain, simple, yet beautiful language characterized the preaching of Martin Luther. He knew how to address himself to the people who heard him in a manner that led them to accept his messages. He believed the gospel should be "prepared plainly and carefully, just as a mother prepares the food for her baby." He once told his students:

When I preach in the Stadt-Kirche I stoop down, I do not look up to the Doctors and the Masters of Arts, of whom there are about forty in my audience, but I look upon the crowd of young people, children, and servants, of whom there are several hundreds. To them I preach. To them I adapt myself. They need it. If the Doctors don't care to hear that style of preaching, the door is open for them to leave.[3]

[1] E. W. Plass, *This Is Luther* (St. Louis: Concordia Publishing House, 1948).
[2] *Luther: The Leader* (New York: Eaton and Mains, 1906), p. 223.
[3] *Ibid.*

He was often carried away with his subject, so that to himself and to many of his hearers his sermons seemed much shorter than they were. His delivery was dynamic. His contemporaries testify to the spell he cast over those who heard him preach. He was eloquent and masterful in his handling of the language, fresh and vigorous in expressing old truths, and clear and interesting in expressing new ones.

In Luther's day, the sermon had become a time for dry dogmatics and scholastic speculations. It occupied a subordinate place in public worship. We can credit the reformer for helping to restore the sermon to its rightful place in the worship service—in its very center.

Martin Luther was doubtless one of those preachers whose written sermons cannot reveal to us the intensity of his soul as he preached them. Those who heard him, even though his plain and sometimes blunt speech offended them, eagerly came again and again to hear his penetrating voice and see the fire flashing from his dark eyes, for they sensed the deep conviction of his soul and were moved by the sincere, urgent intensity of his delivery.

No words here could describe the fervency of his spirit, the courage of his soul, and the eloquence of his lips so well as the words of the last stanza of his great hymn "A Mighty Fortress Is Our God," as translated by F. H. Hedge:

> That word above all earthly powers—
> No thanks to them, abideth;
> The Spirit and the gifts are ours
> Through Him who with us sideth.
> Let goods and kindred go,
> This mortal life also;
> The body they may kill:
> God's truth abideth still,
> His kingdom is forever.

Whatever differences of opinion there may be about Luther, there can be no question as to the extraordinary greatness of the man. His personality can hardly be described as less than immense, and his preaching set a pattern of potency and power for Protestant pulpiteers to follow.

28

CHAPTER 4

Ulrich Zwingli
1484-1531

"Friend Zwingli, thou shalt make the lad a priest."

So said the neighbors of the wealthy farmer and stockman who served as their chief magistrate, and whose son, Ulrich, had demonstrated his ability as a debater, especially on matters of religion.

"Yes," said the thoughtful father. "I have already decided him for the schools."

The mountain-born farmer's son from the village of Wildhaus in the beautiful Toggenburg Valley of Switzerland was on his way to becoming one of the most influential figures among those who brought about the Reformation, for in the forty-seven years of his life he accomplished as much for the Protestant movement as did any man who ever lived.

Ulrich Zwingli was a born controversalist. He took an early interest in contests of all sorts, and he increasingly devoted himself to a search for truth. As a lad, he was remembered for his common sense, his quick wit, and his brilliant mind. He was a precocious boy, but he was also a boy who loved fun. He loved a word-war and enjoyed debate, but he also thrilled to the challenge of physical exercise and athletic contests.

At the age of ten Ulrich Zwingli displayed marks of scholarship far beyond his years, and by the time he had reached the age of twenty he had graduated from the University at Bern. He received his master's degree two years later, and as a young priest he labored enthusiastically and tirelessly.

Like Luther, Zwingli had no intention of beginning a reform movement which would result in his withdrawal from the Roman church. He did not question the pope's authority, but he did exalt the word of God above the traditions of the church. The reactions, of course, came soon enough. He found himself under attack, and he faced the decision which made his ministry what it was. If Rome was to be pagan, then Zwingli and Rome must part company! Amid the jeers of some who said, "This priest of mountain rustics sets himself against popes and cardinals at whose feet emperors have bowed," he stood his ground.

Ulrich Zwingli will be remembered in history as that figure of Reformation courage whose messages were not merely a protest against something, but were rather a positive declaration in favor of something.

He was not so much occupied with error, of which doubtless there was an abundance in his day, but he concerned himself with truth. He fought against darkness, but he did it by means of spreading light. He did not bother to stop and denounce Rome, for he was busy exalting the doctrines of the apostolic Church. Rather than making a business of opposing the sins which prevailed and the corruptions which appeared in the church, he pointed toward the heights of purity which were attainable by all.

His associations with Erasmus during the early days of his ministry helped him strengthen his faith and set his course. There is no doubt that he possessed the experience of full salvation, as a result of his study of the Scriptures, his complete devotion to Christ, and his unswerving faithfulness in performing his task. As he grew in his knowledge of the Scriptures—a knowledge unequaled by others of his time—he grew also in a love of the truth and in a greatness of soul. He often proclaimed such watchwords as: "Christ is our Sacrifice; we need no other!" and, "By one offering he hath perfected for ever them that are sanctified."

While the cathedral preacher at Zurich, Zwingli bravely set his course toward truth and steadily contended for his faith. Boldly and courageously, he introduced changes which brought criticism and opposition upon him, but heralded him as God's man with those who saw the wisdom of his course.

In Zwingli's time only fragmentary portions of the Scriptures were used in connection with the public worship services, and the comments of the priests were greatly lacking in spiritual force and power. Zwingli changed this at Zurich. He hated superficiality, and his soul craved to get at the heart of things. The cathedral at Zurich heard preaching never heard before in that place, and the results were significant. Zwingli was in the Church of Rome, but not of it. He was a Protestant long before he himself knew it.

Although Zwingli and Luther, these two remarkable men raised up by a gracious and merciful God to light the light that was to dispel the darkness of paganism, preached the same doctrines and fought the same battles, they did not meet personally until the work of each was far advanced. Although they had some sharp differences—notably on the Lord's supper—Zwingli often said, "If Luther preaches in Wittenberg the same gospel I preach in Zurich, then I am a Lutheran; if otherwise, I am not."

Zwingli rested his faith on the word of God. His system of doctrine was substantially that of Augustine. His creed was a simple one. He believed that man was holy, but had fallen. Recovery was not his work, but God's. "Christ, very man and very God," he said, "has purchased for us a never ending redemption. His suffering satisfies the divine justice forever in behalf of those who by an unshaken faith rely upon it. If we could have been saved by our works, it would not have been necessary for Christ to die."

He believed in the doctrine of personal election, but unlike some present-day followers of Augustine and Calvin, he did not understand it as being in conflict with man's free agency and accountability to God.

Zwingli rejected appeals to sentimentality. Worship, under his direction, became less aesthetic but more spiritual. He sought for his hearers a more direct contact with God than had been available to them under Roman supervision. Crucifixes and pictures were removed from the walls of the cathedral where he was priest. The church was led to higher planes of spiritual understanding and insight under his ministry.

Ulrich Zwingli was not an orator. He did not possess the impetuous enthusiasm which characterized the preaching of

31

Martin Luther, and he did not reach that moral grandeur which immortalized this Augustinian monk in his impassioned appeal at the Diet of Worms. He did not move audiences as Luther did, but he might well have been a safer guide.

His personal appearance was in his favor, for there was not a more handsome man in Zurich than Zwingli. Tall and strong of body, he spoke with a tone of authority combined with a note of kindness. His voice was clear and sympathetic, and it carried to every corner of the sanctuary when he spoke. Both those who approved and those who disapproved agreed that he was a man of power in the pulpit. His power was born, not of eloquence, but of logic, common sense, keen thinking, and a burning heart.

Zwingli was a sympathetic pastor who enjoyed mingling with the people. Like Paul in Ephesus, he often reasoned with them in the markets of trade; and like the early Christian evangelists, he preached from house to house. The humble recognized in Ulrich Zwingli their friend, and the noble respected him as their sympathetic peer.

Zwingli carefully observed his hours of study, guarding them from all unnecessary intrusions. He never went into his pulpit poorly prepared, and his study habits were reflected in a rich, biblical content of sermons. His own words, concerning his expository style of preaching, were:

The life of Christ has too long been hidden from the people; I shall preach upon the whole of St. Matthew's Gospel, chapter by chapter, according to the inspiration of the Holy Ghost, without human commentaries, drawing solely from the fountain of Scripture, sounding its depths, comparing one passage with another and seeking for understanding by constant and earnest prayer. It is to God's glory, to the praise of His only Son, to the real salvation of souls and to their edification in the true faith, that I shall consecrate my ministry! [1]

A typical sermon of Ulrich Zwingli was the one entitled "The Clarity and Certainty of the Word of God." The

[1] Sample, *op. cit.*, p. 227.

principal criticism of this—and of most of his sermons—is that it is somewhat formless in its composition. The scriptural examples are unnecessarily numerous, and there are in it many exegeses of passages which are not directly related to the main theme. In spite of these homiletical weaknesses there is undoubtedly a fine quality of power and freedom in his development of the subject. There are a vitality of thought and a freshness of expression that were ahead of his day.

A man of learning, a man to be depended upon as a friend, a man of unlimited courage, Ulrich Zwingli met his death at the youthful age of forty-seven in battle at Kappel. He had been faithful to his convictions, faithful to the interests of his country, faithful in his opposition to Rome's use of Swiss mercenaries, and faithful to the preaching of the Word of God, which he loved so well.

With Zwingli, religious zeal was translated into political action and ultimately into fierce physical struggle. His beliefs were to him a "life and death" matter, and indeed he died fighting for them. He seemed to think compulsion might aid his cause, and he became directly involved in the war that resulted from the irreconcilable positions of those who stood against all that the Reformation movement sought to achieve, and the Reformers themselves. When the Zurich canton was attacked, Zwingli rode with the troops as their war chaplain, but he did not confine his energies to their spiritual welfare, he actually fought bravely by the side of men to whom he administered words of comfort and encouragement.

It was while speaking words of consolation into the ears of a dying man on the battlefield that Ulrich Zwingli received his fatal wound. The last words he uttered are typical of a man who carried into every phase of his life the courage of his convictions. He said, "What matters it? They may kill the body, but they cannot kill the soul."

When Ulrich Zwingli died a great light went out in the Church of God. Other reformers were mightier than he by their words, but few were mightier by their actions. With the passing of the years and the dawn of better times, the Church of Jesus Christ has looked back upon his faith and works with utmost favor, for his contribution to the Kingdom will not be measured until the Judge sits upon his throne and the books are opened.

CHAPTER 5

Philip Melanchthon

1497-1560

"What purity and elegance of style! What rare learning! What comprehensive reading! What tenderness and refinement in his extraordinary genius!"

Thus wrote Erasmus in 1516. The object of this extravagant tribute was a lad of nineteen, a lad named Philip Melanchthon.

This youth, the son of honest and pious German parents from Bretton, was never ordained; yet he is recognized as one of the greatest preachers of the Reformation. His ministry was a teaching ministry. He was a brilliant scholar in whom the Protestant movement found an effective ally and the Roman church a formidable opponent. Fourteen years younger than Martin Luther, and a professor in the same University of Wittenberg from the time he was twenty-one years old, he had a warm, friendly relationship with the great Reformation leader from their first acquaintance. His friendship with Luther and their labors together made the winning combination for truth over error, and for vital, living faith over dead, useless form.

Philip Melanchthon's father perhaps did not realize the prophetic accurancy of his dying words to his son: "I have seen many and great changes in the world, but greater ones are yet to follow, in which may God lead you and guide you. Fear God, and do right."

The most distinguishing characteristic of Philip Melanchthon was his ability as a scholar. J. W. Richard, in his biography of Melanchthon, wrote that "in matters of intellect he had a quick perception, an acute penetration, a retentive memory, an ardent thirst for knowledge, and the ability to express his thoughts with accuracy and precision." [1]

[1] *Philip Melanchthon: The Preceptor of Germany* (New York: G. P. Putnam's Sons, 1898).

It will be readily agreed that such a description portrays qualities of a preacher that can make him an effective and useful instrument in the Master's hands. Philip, as a youth, went about asking questions. A common occurrence during his school days was his gathering of several classmates together in an interested little group to discuss what had been read and learned in the classroom.

It was because of his brilliant record as a scholar that his name was changed from the German family name of Schwartzert to its Greek equivalent, Melanchthon.

He attended the Latin school at Pforzheim, the University of Herdeberg, and the University at Tübingen. He studied philosophy, mathematics, natural science, law, medicine, and the Greek and Roman classics. He especially found the latter interesting and helped to kindle a new enthusiasm for these subjects, which had had such a long sleep in the dust of the ages. Melanchthon's influence helped create interest in liberal culture once more among the scholars of Italy, France, England, Holland, and Germany.

Philip Schaff, reformation historian, gives Melanchthon more credit than any of his contemporaries, not excepting Erasmus, for reviving the study of the Greek language and literature. What has all this to do with his contribution as a preacher? The answer is this: The revival of knowledge of the original languages of the Scriptures was an essential service to the cause of biblical learning, and it materially promoted the triumph of the Reformation. Melanchthon called the ancient languages the swaddling clothes of the Christ child; Luther compared them to the sword of the Spirit.

Melanchthon graduated in 1519 with the bachelor of divinity degree; he declined the degree of doctor. At twenty-one he was a professor in the University of Wittenberg, where he was said to have been the most popular professor in the university. It was here that he preached for the benefit of foreign students who did not know German, and his sermons delivered each Sunday in Latin drew audiences of as many as 1,500 to 2,000 people.

Let his contribution as a "teaching minister" he summarized this way: As a model Christian scholar, he combined the highest scientific and literary culture which was attainable in his age with a simple, humble, childlike Christian faith. He had a tough, scientific mind, but a tender, sympathetic heart. He systematized Luther's ideas, defended them in public, and made them a basis of a religious education.

In his early youth, Melanchthon was deeply influenced by the preaching of Father Geiler, his boyhood priest. The younger man came in contact with a devout and pious spirit which did not waste its energies in doubtful speculations and disputations. Geiler rebuked sin and reasoned of "righteousness, temperance, and judgment to come." The young Philip heard preaching that was sincere, straightforward, and powerful. It was delivered in homely and familiar language, and it met everyday problems and needs. Such a background influenced his own concept of preaching, for his ministry followed that pattern until his death.

He was a small man in stature and was plain and unprepossessing in appearance. He was extremely timid, but rather than a handicap this quality was one of his greatest assets. When he spoke, he quickly established empathy with his listeners. Melanchthon looked like a saint. He had a high and noble forehead, and his fine, blue eyes flashed fire as he proclaimed truth. He was not a handsome man, but his outward appearance indicated an inner beauty. His moral character was never questioned and his learning never disputed.

Luther once said of their relationship together in the Reformation movement:

I am rough, boisterous, stormy, and altogether warlike, fighting against innumerable monsters and devils. I am born for the removing of stumps and stones, cutting away thistles and thorns, and clearing the wild forests; but master Philippus comes along softly and gently, sowing and watering with joy, according to the gifts which God has abundantly bestowed upon him.[2]

Without Melanchthon, Luther would have lacked one of

[2] Philip Schaff, *St. Augustine, Melanchthon, Neander* (London: James Nisbet & Company, 1886), p. 114.

his most valuable allies in the struggle for his principles of Reformation. Without Luther, Melanchthon's teaching of Greek might have ended in a higher and purer humanistic culture and perhaps in nothing more. Together, Luther and Melanchthon produced the Protestant movement, changed the course of history, and introduced the modern era. Luther's fiery eloquence and commanding personality brought the Reformation before the people: Melanchthon's moderation, his love of order, and his profound scholarship won for the Reformation the backing of the educated.

Melanchthon was an impressive speaker. Not an orator, he was, nevertheless, interesting. Profound, he was yet a natural speaker with homely, down-to-earth qualities of delivery. The *Schaff-Herzog Encyclopedia* states that he "exerted a wide influence in the department of homiletics, and has been regarded as the author of Protestant methodical style of preaching."

In his method of sermon preparation, Melanchthon insisted on unity and stressed the literal sense of the scripture. He once wrote that whatever is looked for in the words of the Scriptures, outside its literal sense, is only dogmatic or practical application. His approach to preaching was theological and practical, but not essentially grammatical.

One of his sermons, published in the first volume of *The World's Great Sermons,* is on the subject "The Safety of the Virtuous." The text is "Neither shall any man pluck them out of my hand." (John 10:28.)

This sermon was preached to a people who were fearful and anxious in time of national crisis. It contains strong elements of consolation for those who suffer trials and testings and combines keen intellect with warm, sympathetic understanding.

This sermon begins and ends with a prayer and contains many references to the Scriptures. Sin is pictured as a deadly and destructive force let loose upon the world and upon the Church; God's wrath is declared to be righteous and terrible toward evil. Hope is offered through faith in the blood of Jesus Christ.

38

Melanchthon's sermons possessed a characteristic which perhaps could be called imagination. It was the ability to make the absent present. He gave such genuine and living substance to the "hoped for" as to cause it to exercise pull and lift upon the lives of his listeners.

The old prophet Ezekiel set an example for prophets of all time, as John A. Broadus has pointed out. Ezekiel said in the midst of crisis, "I sat where they sat, and remained there astonished among them seven days." He contemplated the whole situation until their doom became his own, and their sorrow became his sorrow. Whatever else we may say of Philip Melanchthon, we must also say that his great, sympathetic soul felt the turmoil of his times. His was a voice crying in the wilderness of corruption, and it helped substantially in the bringing of light and truth through simple faith in Christ, the living Word.

CHAPTER 6

John Knox

1505-72

"O Lord, give me Scotland, or I die!"

John Knox, like Paul, knew how to pray great prayers. He was never known to do anything in a halfhearted manner, and he was most zealous of all when he was engaged in intercessory prayer. His prayers for Scotland were answered, and he is the man recognized by historians as having made a more lasting influence upon his nation's destiny than all others whose lives played a part in its most formative period of years.

John Knox was born in or near Haddington in 1505. His ancestors were feudal dependents of the Earl of Bothwell, and his early education was one of modest proportions in the Haddington grammar school and St. Andrew's University under Major, the famous schoolman of his day. He took minor orders, and about 1540 he appeared as an apostolic notary at Haddington.

Knox embraced the reformed faith after having heard George Wishart, the martyr, preach in East Lothian in December of 1545. After the murder of Cardinal Beaton, Wishart's persecutor, John Knox fled to the castle of St. Andrews and soon began preaching to those in the garrison. It is easy to see, in view of the background and early beginnings of his ministry, why John Knox could never separate his preaching of the gospel from the political issues of the day. He believed good government and good religion should work together, and his ministry was aimed toward a strengthening of both.

Impetuous, courageous, and firm in all his dealings with men, John Knox was nevertheless the possessor of a frail body. One of his contemporaries, not of the Protestant faith, said of him: "I know not if ever so much piety and genius were lodged in such a frail and weak body. Certain I am, that it will be difficult to find one in whom the gifts of the Holy Spirit shone so bright to the comfort of the church in Scotland." [1]

Knox was below average in height, but was straight and well proportioned. His complexion was swarthy, yet was not unpleasant to look upon. His countenance was grave and stern, yet not harsh, and bore a natural dignity and an air of authority. His black eyes, black hair, and rather dense brows gave his eyes the appearance of having receded into hollows. When he preached with intense feeling his eyes reflected the power of his personality, and his manner became imperious. He wore a beard during most of his public life, and it varied in length from year to year. Some of the portraits of the Scottish pulpiteer indicate that his beard was long enough to hang down almost to the pages of the Bible from which he read his texts.

Enoch Pond has said that in John Knox the love of study was combined with a disposition for active employment. This combination of character qualities is rare but excellent. Knox became trained in all branches of learning by his formal education and his habits of private study and adaptation. He found no satisfaction in his studies of all the theories of scholastic science.

To read the sermons of John Knox is to be convinced that they were carefully prepared. He did not wander from the subject matter of his text and theme, but diligently developed his proposition and logically progressed with his thought.

Knox usually gave his outline to the congregation at the beginning of his message, and the use of his "firstly," "secondly," and "thirdly" made it easy for them to follow him as he developed it. His outline for his sermon on "The First Temptation of Christ" was:

I. What this word temptation meaneth, and how it is used within the Scriptures.

[1] Thomas McCrie, *The Life of John Knox* (New York: Eastman, Kirk & Company, 1813), p. 376.

II. Who is here tempted, and at what time this temptation happened.

III. How and by what means He was tempted.

IV. Why He should suffer these temptations and what fruits ensue to us from the same.[2]

John Knox, being the devout man of prayer that he was, depended upon the power of prayer in preparing his sermons. He read from both the Old and New Testaments daily, and each day included in his devotional reading some portions of the Psalms.

Knox has been called by some "a Hebrew Prophet in sixteenth century Scotland." In the prophetic ministry of "forthtelling" he excelled as one who believed the truth of the message he proclaimed. In the other meaning of prophecy, "foretelling," he also dared to proclaim the truth as he believed it. Many, if not all, of his predictions happened just as he said they would. Knox himself claimed the power of prophecy, when he said, "I dare not deny, lest that in so doing I should be injurious to the Giver, that God hath revealed to me secrets unknown to the world." [3]

Knox's zeal and enthusiasm in the pulpit were marks of distinction for the ministry of the man. He was known on some occasions to proceed with his preaching appointment even when his health was poor and his strength was so weak that he had to be helped to the platform. McCrie was correct in saying, "Preaching was an employment in which he delighted."

John Knox used frequent gestures. A young student who heard him preach said of his delivery that he was so active and vigorous in the pulpit that he was "likely to beat the pulpit to pieces."

Once deciding for or against a matter, Knox felt very keenly about it and expressed himself as he felt. His passions were strong, and his zeal at times led him to use intemperate

---

[2] Grenville Kleiser (comp.), *The World's Great Sermons* (New York: Funk & Wagnalls Company, 1908), p. 173.

[3] William Croft Dickenson (ed.), *John Knox's History of the Reformation in Scotland* (New York: Philosophical Library, Inc., 1950).

language. His reproofs were usually vigorous and positive, and often irritated those he sought to reclaim.

His voice varied with the content of his messages. At times, he spoke in a moderate tone of voice much like the conversational tone heard today, but as his enthusiasm rose and his climax came, his voice became louder, with its pitch and tone increasing in intensity as he gestured energetically. When John Knox preached, as when he prayed, he did so with all the energy, the potency, and the vigor that he could command.

His illustrations as such were not like those commonly used today. He seldom used a narrative as an illustration, but he had a way of weaving the material into his message. The most common source of his illustrative material was the Bible. From its history, incidents, and personalities he often illustrated his points.

The Scottish wit having the reputation that it has, Knox would be expected to possess his share of a sense of humor. This he did, as some of his sermons so keenly reflect.

His dry wit found its way into his messages, and often became the vehicle upon which his enthusiastic displeasure rode into the hearts and minds of his listeners. A favorite activity of his seemed to be ridiculing the priests. An example is found in his description of the tumult and confusion in the church on St. Giles' Day. He said of it: "For down goes the crosses, off goes the surplices, round caps corner with the crowns. The Grey Friars gaped, the Black Friars blew, the priests panted and fled; and happy was he that first got to the house, for such a sudden fray came never among the generation of antichrist with this realm before." [4]

With short, adroit phrases Knox often punctured alike the tough and tender skins of his adversaries. He spoke of Bishop Sinclair of Brechin as being "blind of one eye in the body, but of both in the soul." He once said of Lady Erskine that she was "a sweet morsel for the devil's mouth." His

[4] *Ibid.*

comment upon the appointment of Mary of Guise as queen regent was, "It is as seemly a sight as to put a saddle upon the back of an unruly cow."

His humor was doubtless a God-given attribute; for it not only stood him in good stead in his parries with those who opposed his reforms for his native Scotland, but it also held him steady in the balance of his personality against the zeal that possessed him. There is little doubt that his sense of humor, which he enjoyed even when it was at his own expense, saved him from going into fanaticism as a result of his earnestness and zeal.

His wit, keen as it was, did not always characterize his preaching, however. There was a serious current flowing through his sermons and his entire ministry. He was ardent, acute, intrepid, and energetic; he was active and courageous; he was vigorous and impetuous; he was enthusiastic at times to the point of vehemence. He could move his audiences to weeping as well as to laughter. At the funeral of Regent Moray, who was assassinated by Hamilton, he preached from the text "Blessed are the dead that die in the Lord," and three thousand hearers were moved to tears.

Mary, Queen of Scots, once said that she feared the prayers of John Knox more than the armies of England. Her fears were well founded, for his prayers and his preaching were powerful enough to snatch Scotland from the influence of the Roman Catholic Church in spite of the opposition of the church and the authority of the queen. May there be more such praying and preaching to lead our own nation into the revival she needs in this twentieth century.

CHAPTER 7

John Calvin

1509-64

> *"Tot verba, tot pondera.* Every
> word weighed a pound!"

So spoke Beza, and so agreed the congregations. No other statement could describe so well in so few words the heart of John Calvin's preaching. Calvin is remembered primarily for his doctrines, but he should also be remembered as one of the great examples of expository preachers during Reformation times.

Born in Noyon, Picardy, in 1509, this physically weak little Frenchman was an infant when Zwingli and Luther were already twenty-five and twenty-six years of age. In spite of his lateness in point of time, he must be ranked among the most influential leaders in the great religious struggle of the sixteenth century.

With his gentle birth and extensive education, Calvin prepared himself for a law career at the insistence of his father. After his father's death, he turned his interests toward the classics and eventually toward the Christian faith. His words express the change in his interest: "What is the use of seeking information from the pagan philosophers, when they contradict each other?" At the age of twenty-five, the Bible had become his main source book.

John Broadus once said that a great preacher "is not a mere artist, and not a feeble suppliant, he is a conquering soul, a monarch, a born ruler of mankind." The preacher's task is to will and to cause men to bow. Calvin's strong character gave force to his utterance, and this unusual forcefulness was intensified by his saturation in the word of God.

John Calvin's general preparation was more than adequate, but such authorities as Andrew W. Blackwood have commented on his seeming weakness in specific preparation for a particular sermon. Blackwood said of

45

him that he "did not always take time to prepare his expository discourses with care, and he seldom revised them in detail." In spite of this candid appraisal of a fundamental weakness, there is sufficient merit in Calvin's preaching to draw from his critics the praise he deserved. After all, he preached daily for months at a stretch. His general study habits and his unusual memory span and powers of retention apparently succeeded in atoning for his haste in sermon building.

Williston Walker, in his biography of John Calvin, described the long hours he spent in his study. He slept little, and by five or six o'clock in the morning his books were brought to him in bed. Much of the morning was spent in bed with his books. Because of a consumptive, asthmatic condition, he thought a reclining position better for his health. After the single meal which constituted his daily diet in his later years, he often walked about in his room for a quarter of an hour. Then he returned to his studies.

His few recreations were briefly enjoyed. He was not disposed to good-humored small talk and seldom interrupted his study for relaxation, even though his friends insisted.

Leroy Nixon, while a student of homiletics under Professor Blackwood at Princeton, made a study of Calvin's preaching. He concluded that Calvin gave the soundest, ablest, clearest expositions of scripture that had been seen in a thousand years. Calvin's exegeses were sound, and were pursued with loving zeal. He had a unique ability to see quickly the exact relationship of many scattered portions of scripture.

Calvin's attitude toward biblical preaching, in his own words, was that God's word had been committed to the preachers "like the royal sceptre of God, under which all creatures bow their heads and bend their knees." He advised:

Let them boldly dare all things, and constrain all the glory, highness, and power of this world to obey and to yield to the divine majesty; let them by this same Word have command over everyone; let them edify the house of Christ, overthrowing the

46

reign of Satan; let them lead the flock to pasture and kill the wolves; let them bind and let loose thunder and lightning, if that is their calling, but all in God's Name.[1]

John Calvin drew all his sermons from the Bible. He preached from it as he found it, book by book and passage by passage. Calvin attempted to show clearly and strongly what the Scriptures meant and what difference they ought to make in the hearts and lives of his hearers. He did not "go everywhere preaching the gospel," but rather stayed by the passage at hand.

The force in John Calvin's preaching unquestionably came from the fact that his mind and heart were saturated by the word of God.

Calvin was able, as it suited him, to set his own unique style of homiletics. He had no introduction, as a rule. "We saw yesterday" or "We have seen this morning" were typical beginnings and constituted all the introduction his sermon needed.

"Therefore, we see now" or "We will have to save the rest until tomorrow" were typical conclusions.

As for divisions, transitions, and other homiletical devices, there is little evidence that he paid any attention to them. "That is the second thing we must note," "So much for one item," or "This is what we must conclude from this passage" perhaps came nearest to serving as transitional phrases. Little attention was paid to appearance or filling in; every word served for application, for edification, for substantial reality. Such forms as are found present in the analysis of Calvin's sermons are apparently due, not to conscious art, but to his logically trained mind. There are no illustrations from literature.

His appearance was against him, for he was not a handsome man. Narrow lips and sunken eyes in a great head mounted upon a weak body yet seemed to command respect as he stood before his hearers. He spoke slowly and de-

[1] Leroy Nixon, *John Calvin, Expository Preacher* (Grand Rapids, Mich.: William B. Eerdmans Publishing Company, 1959), p. 58.

liberately, so that anyone wishing to take notes had ample time to do so as his sermon progressed. He did not have a good voice, and sometimes asthma caused a decidedly unpleasant rasp. What, then, made him a great preacher? The answer must be that he always had something to say, and that he used the language of the Holy Spirit, without ornamentation, without attempts at oratorical or rhetorical beauty, yet with the force and power found only in the word!

The courage and spirit which brought John Calvin through days of personal tragedy and danger are much more admirable than his doctrinal beliefs, especially by those in the holiness movement. In fairness to Calvin, however, it should be pointed out that many of the extreme tenets of "Calvinism" are the interpretations some of Calvin's followers placed upon his teachings, rather than Calvin's own words. In Calvin's preaching the primary truth is the sovereignty of God. God is Master. Nothing happens except at his command. He has the right to command and to expect obedience. His interest, his glory, and his honor must have first place in our lives.

Eternal election, or God's predestination of some to salvation and others to destruction, is a corollary of the doctrines of the absolute sovereignty of God, and at this point some disagree with Calvin's conclusions. John Calvin himself preached a positive assurance in this particular tenet of his doctrinal system, but many of his followers have made a negative approach in their interpretation of this problem. Looking back upon Calvin's ministry from the vantage point of these succeeding centuries, it would seem that perhaps God's purpose was served through the unwavering belief this man had that he was one of God's elect and therefore could not fail, for indeed the tragedies in his life and the sufferings in his own experiences were such that he may well have turned aside had he not found the comfort he needed in his concept of God as the sovereign Ruler and Master of the universe. Calvin was right in placing his trust in a God whom he believed would not fail him!

Nixon made four applications to our preaching for today when he concluded his study of John Calvin's ministry. First, be a real student of the Bible. Second, preach often. Third, appeal to the deepest needs of the congregation. Fourth, speak plainly; be conversational, not oratorical.

Preachers should desire to preach the truth in living freshness, and a knowledge of the Bible is fundamental. All the art of rhetoric is useless if the content of the sermon is thin or shallow. The preaching of John Calvin demonstrated that force and power are assured when the Scriptures are honored and the Holy Spirit anoints.

When John Calvin preached, the people did not go from the church saying, "Wasn't that a fine sermon?" or, "Is he not a wonderful preacher?" They said rather what might be hoped by every preacher they may say of him: "Truly, he speaks the word of God. We must live by it if we would know God's blessings and be assured of his love and favor."

CHAPTER 8

Jonathan Edwards
1703-58

When Jonathan Edwards preached on July 8, 1741, on the subject "Sinners in the Hands of an Angry God," his audience groaned and shrieked convulsively until their outcries of distress for their souls drowned the preacher's voice, and he was forced to pause while the crowd quieted. This message added the spark of fire that sent a revival spirit sweeping across eighteenth-century New England.

"I think a person of moral responsibility, alone at midnight, reading that awful discourse, would well-nigh go crazy," said Henry C. Fish in *Pulpit Eloquence* as he described this sermon later. "He would hear the judgment trump, and see the advancing heaven, and the day of doom would begin to mantle him with its shroud." [1]

This is the picture of Jonathan Edwards that many people have seen. In the light of recent studies, however, Edwards is seen more as a man who denounced like a Calvinist but had the compassion of an Arminian. Studies now being presented in the Yale edition of the *Works of Jonathan Edwards,* edited by Perry Miller, Paul Ramsay, John E. Smith, Thomas C. Schafer, John H. Gerstner, and others (some of which is in publication and much of which will be published later) shows a better understanding of the preaching emphasis of Jonathan Edwards. These scholars see Edwards as a preacher whose strongly negative evangelistic sermons were one side, but only one side, of his preaching. He dwelt much on the love of God, the joys of heaven, the conduct of the Christian life, and the religious import of public events. His preaching was designed to build up the saints as well as to convert the sinners.

Jonathan Edwards' father, Timothy Edwards, was the

---

[1] *Pulpit Eloquence* (New York: Dodd, Mead & Company, 1856), p. 395.

minister for sixty years at Windsor, Connecticut, where Jonathan was born in 1703. The only son, Jonathan, was reared with a family of ten sisters in a strictly religious environment of hard work and thrifty economy.

It was this sort of life that Edwards lived during his first thirteen years. In many ways, he was fortunate, for he missed some of the pitfalls that waited in the path of those who had a less pious environment, and he gained an advantage from the isolation of his early life. The beauty of nature, the simplicity of the good life, and the security of a large Christian household doubtless made an impression upon him in his formative years.

Ola Elizabeth Winslow quoted a letter that he wrote to his sister when he was just a boy. "In the news of the revival with which he begins," she commented, "he talks more like a deacon than a twelve-year-old boy; but with his own awakening behind him he was already on the side of the pulpit and yearning toward the unconverted." [2]

As early as the age of seven, Jonathan Edwards experienced what can be described most accurately as a crisis of regenerating grace. He expressed his own feelings later as a raptness before the majesty and holiness of God which caused his heart to yearn "to lie low before God, as in the dirt that I might be all, that I might become as a little child." Sharing in the awakened fervor of the village church in which his father preached, the lad found a secluded spot in a wooded area where he led other children in moments of prayer.

A freshman in New Haven College at the age of thirteen, Edwards transferred to Weathersfield after the first year and graduated in 1720. These colleges were both a part of Yale University, where he continued his education in the school of theology and later taught until a long illness interrupted his work.

It was in his twenty-three years as the pastor of the Congregational Church in Northampton that his ministry

[2] *Jonathan Edwards* (New York: The Macmillan Company, 1940), p. 49.

proved most fruitful. Revival after revival swept through his church and community during his ministry there. His work there came to an end when he left his pulpit rather than to compromise in his convictions. His penetrating and discomfiting rebukes of sin and his refusal to allow the unconverted to participate in the Lord's Supper led to his dismissal. He then became president of Princeton College. He died a month later at the age of fifty-five.

This is the man; what was he like in the pulpit? Robert Hall said of him, "He ranks with the brightest luminaries of the Christian Church." Henry C. Fish praised him, "Edwards has been rarely, if ever, excelled since the days of the Apostles." His ability was most certainly not to be found in his voice, his eloquence, or his style of delivery. His manner was not oratorical or flowery. His voice was not unusually pleasant or strong; on the contrary it was weak and unattractive. His strength lay in the richness of thought and the overwhelming power of argument in his appeal to the minds and the hearts of his listeners.

Edwards' eyesight was poor, and he read his sermons from a manuscript. These facts put together suggest the picture of a nearsighted preacher holding his manuscript close to his face as he reads his sermon with painstaking care. In the poor light of a dim, dark sanctuary, he held a candle in one hand while he clutched his papers in the other!

It is unbelievable that such style of delivery could have conveyed the content of his sermons with such power. But there was something about his preaching that struck deep into the consciences of his listeners, and whatever that "something" was, it is something every preacher should cultivate.

Harwood Pattison, in *The History of Christian Preaching*, described Edwards' preaching style:

With the manuscript held close to his eyes, gesture was almost impossible. The preacher's voice was not attractive, and he had no graces of manner which could commend him to his hearers. His style was rugged rather than careless, but it never failed to express his thought in clear and telling language. Argumentative he was, but not for the sake of argument; logical, but only under the resistless impulse of the highest reason; doctrinal, and yet not so much for the sake of doctrine as for the sake of its application. His intellect was not cold although it might be calm, it was fired with intense conviction.[3]

"Sinners in the Hands of an Angry God" was preached from the text in Deut. 32:35: "Their foot shall slide in due time." He used words so real and alive that if you could have cut them they would have bled. For example:

The devils watch them, they are ever by them, at their right hand; they stand waiting for them, like greedy, hungry lions that see their prey, and expect to have it, but are for the present kept back; if God should withdraw His hand by which they are restrained, they would in a moment fly upon their poor souls.[4]

In the midst of such extreme emotional intensity as his preaching brought, Jonathan Edwards stood quietly and calmly, seemingly unmoved, while his hearers sobbed and screamed in fear of hell. The ability to remain calm seemed significant of a reserve of power within the wasted form and thin voice of the one who seemed to be speaking from the gate of death. There must have been a fearful piercing in the look of his eye when raised from the manuscript, for on one occasion, according to Pattison, it was said that he "looked off" the bell rope in the steeple so that the bell fell with a crash into the church. That such a fantasy should be experienced is a testimony as to the superstitions of the people of his time, but it is also a suggestion as to the extreme emotional intensity resulting from his preaching.

This was only one side of the preaching of Jonathan Edwards, however. He not only preached such sermons as "Wrath upon the Wicked to the Uttermost," but he also preached on such themes as "The Christian Pilgrim," from the text "These all died in the faith, not having received the promises, but having seen them afar off, and were

[3] Philadelphia: The Judson Press, 1903, p. 355.
[4] *Works*, Vol. II.

persuaded of them, and embraced them, and confessed that they were strangers and pilgrims on the earth. For they that say such things declare plainly that they seek a country." (Heb. 11:13-14.)

Few men have been able to weave into their sermons more of the text than Edwards did. His introduction in "The Christian Pilgrim" began: "The Apostle is here setting forth the excellencies of the grace of faith, by the glorious effects and happy issue of it in the saints of the Old Testament." Then he proceeded with a brief explanation of the context and two observations about the text: (1) What these saints confessed of themselves—that they were strangers and pilgrims on the earth; and (2) The inference that the apostle draws from hence—that they sought another country as their home.

The reader notices few breaks in the movement of the message. The outlines in many of Edwards' sermons are not clearly discernible, for his transitions are so smooth as to be unnoticed. Such smooth continuity is one of the characteristics of his style. There are no noticeable breaks between points, between introduction and body, or between body and conclusion.

The text is often repeated in the sermon—perhaps in every paragraph—but not merely for the sake of repetition or emphasis. It is tied in with what is being said, and the reader, as did the hearers, feels the impact of "thus saith the Lord" in what is proclaimed.

Edwards' illustrations are almost entirely in the form of brief comparisons. There are few, if any, anecdotes, but frequent associations, similes, and metaphors. He said: "We should travel in this way in a laborious manner. Long journeys are attended by toil and fatigue; especially if through a wilderness. . . . So we should travel in the way of holiness, improving our time and strength, to surmount the obstacles and difficulties that are in the way." [5]

[5] Andrew W. Blackwood, *The Protestant Pulpit* (Nashville: Abingdon Press, 1947), p. 42.

One of his hearers said his sermons were "more terrible than Dante's *Inferno*." Another of his listeners, John Greenleaf Whittier, wrote a poem expressing his esteem of "the little giant," with a conception of self as minute and love for others as gigantic. Such a pulpit master as F. W. Robertson professed the influence of Edwards' ministry upon his own life to be definite and abiding. A. M. Fairbairn declared that none could dispute Edwards' "claim to stand amid the great thinkers of the world." Pattison points out that his greatness as a preacher is to be found in himself—gravity of character, spiritual insight, vivid imagination, a philosophical grasp of his subject, logical clearness, and a rare combination of masterful will and great tenderness. Richard Neiderhiser, after an extensive study of his life and ministry, observed that many ministers "could well take Jonathan Edwards for an example of sincerity, a tower of spiritual faith, and an expression of true humility."

Edwards will be remembered for his leading role, with the Tennent brothers, in the Great Awakening, and for his profound learning and tremendous stature as a theologian and philosopher. It is unfortunate that so few students of preaching have been able to look beyond the mood and tone of his widely publicized sermons on the wrath of God and the sinner's doom. Shafer and Turnbull have done much to put his preaching in better perspective.

An excellent summary of Jonathan Edwards' philosophy of preaching is seen in the last statement he made just before his death in 1758: "Trust in God, and ye need not fear." In God he did trust, and he lived, preached, and died unafraid.

CHAPTER 9

John Wesley

1703-91

Hot, tired, thirsty, and impatient, the English nobleman asked a peasant, "Why is it that I can't find a place where I can buy a drink of liquor in this wretched village?" The humble peasant, seeing the rank of his questioner, respectfully and courteously replied, "Well, you see, my lord, about a hundred years ago, a man named John Wesley came preaching in these parts."

Perhaps no Englishman who ever lived has had as great an influence upon the history of his nation, or indeed upon the lives of people in every nation, as John Wesley. F. J. McConnell, John Hampson, Maximin Piette, and other biographers agree that, with the possible exception of a few statesmen and a general or two, John Wesley has received more attention from the pens of biographers and has had more written about him than any other Englishman of the eighteenth century. France had no Wesley, and France had her bloody revolution. Britain, with her Wesley, had an eighteenth-century Wesleyan revival, and there was no bloody revolution. The preaching of John Wesley—the Wesley with the warmed heart—gives hope and faith to those who sometimes wonder whether or not much lasting good is accomplished by "the foolishness of preaching."

John Wesley's family background was devoutly religious. He was brought up in a Christian family. His father was a clergyman in the Church of England, and Susanna Wesley, his mother, although busy with the care of nineteen children, found time to give each of them the loving attention and careful Christian nurture that would provide rich, fertile ground for gospel seed. Young John was impressed with her teaching of the importance of keeping the commandments of God, and even as a child he accepted them and tried to apply them in his outward conduct.

After some years at Oxford University, he was persuaded by his father to be ordained as a Christian minister, and this brought a new mood of seriousness into his life. He set apart an hour each day for private prayer and thought, took the sacrament of Holy Communion each week, and set himself to conquer every sin. "Doing so much, and living so good a life, I doubted not but I was a good Christian," is the verdict he himself passed on his life at that time.

He wanted to do still more in the service of God, and he cut out of his life all pleasures and extravagances. He observed fasts twice a week. He visited the prisons and assisted the poor and the sick. Yet, he later explained, when he stood face to face with death, this religion of his gave him little comfort, nor did it afford him the assurance of his acceptance of God.

He volunteered to serve as a missionary in Georgia, in America, but after several years of service returned home unhappy and miserable. A period of illness followed, and he was apprehensive as he thought death was approaching. Then, at a meeting in Aldersgate Street, the truth he had accepted flooded in upon his whole being. He described this experience in his *Journal:*

In the evening I went very unwillingly to a society in Aldersgate Street where one was reading Luther's preface to the Epistle to the Romans. About a quarter before nine, while he was describing the change which God works in the heart through faith in Christ, I felt my heart strangely warmed. I felt I did trust in Christ, Christ alone, for salvation; and an assurance was given me, that He had taken away my sins, even mine, and saved me from the law of sin and death.[1]

From that day until his death, John Wesley—the Wesley of the warmed heart—went about preaching the richness of the Christian experience in its fullness. He preached to those who were "less than full Christians" and challenged them to seek a deep peace, a real enjoyment of faith, happiness in God, joy in the Holy Spirit, a new victory over the power of

[1] May 24, 1738.

evil in their lives, and "an intense, glad eagerness to be utterly obedient to every wish of our Lord." He preached as only a man filled with the Holy Spirit could preach.

First and most important in our analysis of Wesley's preaching is our acknowledgment of its biblical content. His own statement regarding his opinion of the importance of the Bible in his ministry was rigidly observed. He said:

> I have thought I am a creature of a day, passing through life as an arrow through the air. I am a spirit come from God. . . . I want to know one thing—the way to heaven; how to land safely on that happy shore. God himself has condescended to teach the way: for this very end He came from heaven. He hath written it down in a book. O give me that book! At any price give me the book of God! I have it: here is knowledge enough for me. Let me be *homo unius libri*.[2]

John Wesley was certainly the "man of one Book" in the sense that to him the Bible was central. He knew it as few men who have ever lived, and he preached its truth clearly and effectively to all who would hear him. But he was also a man of many books, for his wide reading in the sciences, philosophies, and politics are notable.

In his sermon on the subject "Scriptural Christianity," from the text in Acts 4:31, "And they were all filled with the Holy Ghost," we find an excellent example of the scriptural content in his preaching.[3] There are exactly 109 quotations from the Bible in this one sermon, some from the Old Testament and many from the New Testament, and not one was improperly or inaccurately quoted!

In further examination of the biblical content of Wesley's preaching, it is observed that most of his introductions were biblical and textual. In the sermon just mentioned, for example, he begins by saying, "The same expression occurs in the second chapter, where we read, 'When the day of Pentecost was fully come, they were all' (the Apostles, with

[2] *Works*, vol. 4.
[3] E. H. Sugden, ed., *Standard Sermons of John Wesley* (London: The Epworth Press, 1956), I, 87-111.

the women, and the mother of Jesus, and His brethren) 'with one accord in one place.' " He quoted scriptures from the context and from companion texts and proceeded to excite the interest and "whet the appetites" of his listeners for the exposition of the written word.

His illustrations also were almost entirely taken from biblical sources. Rarely if ever do we find illustrative materials from his own experiences, and only occasionally do we observe illustrations from history and literature. He seemed to enjoy reading the poetry of Homer, and he often quoted from these writings in illustrating his sermons. In his sermon "The Almost Christian" he stated:

> By sincerity I mean, a real, inward principle of religion, from whence these outward actions flow. And, indeed, if we have not this, we have not heathen honesty; no, not so much of it as will answer the demand of a heathen Epicurean poet. Even this poor wretch, in his sober intervals, is able to testify,
> *Oderunt peccare boni, virtutis amore;*
> *Oderunt peccare mali, formidine poenae.*
> [The good hate to sin through love of virtue; you, on the contrary, commit no crime that will tell against you through dread of punishment.] [4]

An examination of Wesley's sermons reveals an extraordinary ability to think clearly and logically and to present truth, controversial though it may be, plainly and convincingly.

Wesley had a closer kinship with Calvin than some have seen, for like Calvin—and like Luther—Wesley's power was centered largely in the principle of "justification by faith." This was in direct opposition to the formalism of Anglicanism and was just as diametrically opposed to his own former moralism, which brought him frustration and failure in Georgia. This justification is always accompanied by regeneration, and its good works are the fruit of the Spirit rather than the fruit of self-righteousness. This is evangelical preaching as it should be!

[4] *Ibid.*, p. 58.

In answering objections in his sermon on "Salvation by Faith," Wesley argued:

Yet, to the same truth, placed in another view, a quite contrary objection is made: "If a man cannot be saved by all that he can do, this will drive men to despair." True, to despair of being saved by their own works, their own merits or righteousness. And so it ought; for none can trust in the merits of Christ, till he has utterly renounced his own! [5]

His outline for this sermon was logically developed:

I. What Faith It Is Through Which We Are Saved.
II. What Is the Salvation Which Is Through Faith?
III. How We May Answer Some Objections. [6]

Clear, simple, rugged, and convincing, this and his other sermons are the practice of what he advised others concerning their preaching. He wrote:

Let your whole deportment before your congregation be serious and weighty and solemn. Always suit your subject to your audience. Choose the plainest texts you can. Take care not to ramble; but keep to your text, and make out what you take in hand. . . . Take care of anything awkward or affected, either in your gesture, phrase, or pronunciation. . . . Beware of clownishness, either in speech or dress. Wear no slouched hat. [7]

He even gave advice concerning the care of the preacher's horse. He said, "Be merciful to your beast. Not only ride moderately, but see with your own eyes that your horse be fed, rubbed, and bedded." This, of course, is obsolete in our day, and yet it might be adapted in some way to our conduct. Who knows—were he living today he perhaps would give advice to his preachers on the care of their cars, or, more to the point, the manner in which they drive their cars.

Mr. Curnock, with Wesley in the morning services in Bristol in 1741, described his preparation for preaching:

[5] *Ibid.*, pp. 48-49.
[6] *Ibid.*, p. 38.
[7] *Works*, vol. 8.

"For this duty he prayed and robed. Usually he went fasting. Returning to his rooms, he drank chocolate or tea, and at once proceeded to write in his journal, or in sermon form, or in a paper for use in society meetings, the substance of the exposition that morning given." [8]

One of the students who heard his sermon at St. Mary's, Oxford, was Benjamin Kennicott, who described his appearance and his sermon in a most revealing manner. Kennicott, no Methodist and no friend of Wesley, said of him later:

"When he mounted the pulpit, I fixed my eyes on him and his behaviour. He is neither tall nor fat; for the latter would ill become a Methodist. His black hair quite smooth, and parted very exactly" [yes, Mr. Kennicott; this man had a way of doing things "very exactly"], "added to a peculiar composure in his countenance, showed him to be an uncommon man. . . . And now he began to exalt his voice. . . . Under these three heads he expressed himself like a very good scholar, but a rigid zealot; and then he came to what he called his plain, practical conclusion. . . . And he fired his address with so much zeal and unbounded satire as quite spoiled what otherwise might have been turned to a great advantage." [9]

John Wesley had a way of making an impression on his listeners, and whether the result was conviction and persuasion or antagonism and anger, they were not the same after having heard him preach. He frequently used a series of rapid-fire, heart-searching, personal questions to achieve this result—as he did in the sermon described by the student Kennicott.

To persuade men to accept and practice "the truth as it is in Jesus" was John Wesley's primary purpose in preaching. To triumph over his adversaries was an ambition far beneath his character, although he was skilled in the presentation of controversial issues. To convince men of error and to induce them to embrace the truth was a purpose of

[8] W. L. Doughty, *John Wesley, the Preacher* (London: The Epworth Press, 1955).
[9] Sugden, *op. cit.*, p. 89.

supreme importance with him. With Wesley, theory was worth nothing unless it should lead to correct practice. He was pre-eminently a practical preacher of the Word of God.

He preached in Saint Mary's in Oxford; he preached in the churches; he preached in the mines; he preached in the fields and on the streets; and he preached on horseback, 20,000 miles a year, reading out of his saddlebags. He even preached on his father's tombstone. He preached the Bible as a man who has studied it carefully and prayerfully. He preached with a note of victory as only a man can preach when he has suffered with his own doubts until he himself has found assurance and victory. He resisted formalism and demanded sincerity. With a heart "strangely warmed" he sounded the bugle of full salvation—"Christian Perfection, properly so called" and perfect love shed abroad in the heart by the Holy Ghost.

They said of him, "He acts as though he were out of breath in pursuit of souls!" May his spirit, his emphasis, and his message so possess those who live and preach the doctrine he believed that the same may be said of all of them.

CHAPTER 10

George Whitefield
1714-70

"Oh, the righteousness of Jesus
Christ! I must be excused if I men-
tion it in almost all my sermons!"

Thus did George Whitefield characterize the emphasis of
his preaching, and thus he perhaps unconsciously explained
the success of his ministry. If there is any one thing that
can account for the tremendous impact of the preaching of
evangelist Whitefield upon the people of his generation, it
is that ᴵ‑‑ ʲreaching was Christ-centered. He exalted Jesus
Christ with unlimited zeal, with unbounded love, and with
unequᴬᴵᴬᵈ ᴵᵏill.

Born in Gloucester, England, in 1714, his early life was
irreligious. His own pamphlet, published in 1740, provides
the only account of his early life and indicates that his
feelings concerning his youth are those of regret that he did
not find conversion earlier than he did.

Whitefield at first resisted the call of God to preach,
but was ordained at twenty-two—still not enthusiastic but
at least willing to give his life to the work of the ministry
of the gospel. The ordination service itself seemed to provide
a spark that had been lacking before; he said later that the
bishop's hand on his head "melted" his heart down. With
a melted heart he preached with eloquence that few
preachers of history have equaled, and none had surpassed.
A. S. Billingsley in his biography of Whitefield wrote that
his eloquence "burst upon the world like a volcanic eruption,
like torrents of red-hot lava it carried everything before it."

Whitefield arrived in Philadelphia in 1739, and none other
than Benjamin Franklin described in his own autobiography
some of the eventful days that followed his first sermons
there. "He was at first permitted to preach in some of our
churches," Franklin wrote, "but the clergy, taking a dislike

63

to him, soon refused him their pulpits, and he was obliged to preach in the fields."

The Philadelphia printer, who was later to become America's first great statesman, soon became a fast friend of Whitefield. Although there is no record that he was one of Whitefield's converts, he held the great evangelist in high esteem and was definitely influenced by his ministry.

Franklin, noted for his frugality, gives a most interesting side light in his *Autobiography* concerning the effect Whitefield's oratory had upon him—as indeed it had upon everyone. Attending a meeting at which Whitefield was to preach, and after which Whitefield was to receive an offering of cash for some worthy project, Franklin recalled:

I silently resolved he should get nothing from me. . . . As he proceeded, I began to soften and concluded to give the coppers [in my pocket]. Another stroke of his oratory made me ashamed of that, and determined me to give the silver; and he finished so admirably that I emptied my pocket wholly into the collector's dish, gold and all.

In appearance, George Whitefield was large and portly and not particularly handsome. He wore a large wig and preached in the gowns such as were worn by the clergy of the Church of England.

In content, Whitefield's sermons were biblical; some were expository, few were topical, many were textual. His introductions were long; many would say they were too long. His sentences were often long and involved, but they were frequently punctuated and usually characterized with short, pungent phrases which made them clear to his listeners. The most striking thing observed in the reading of his published sermons is the skill with which he makes his transitions. Such expressions as "first, then," "but further," "further," "but then," "once more," and the like keep the reader aware of the logical divisions in his outline of thought without making him weary of the monotony of Whitefield's style.

It must be said, however, that reading the published sermons of George Whitefield is likely to be a disappointment for anyone who expects to be impressed because of

Whitefield's reputation as an orator. His oratorical skill is due almost entirely to his ability in extemporaneous speaking and does not appear in his written manuscripts.

What, then, was unusual about the delivery of George Whitefield? For one thing, he possessed a voice such as few men have ever been able to use in their preaching. Joseph Belcher, in *A Biography of George Whitefield*, said his voice could be heard clearly at the distance of a mile in ideal weather conditions. Clara McLeister wrote in her book *Men and Women of Deep Piety;* "His voice . . . was smooth, variable, and could express the gentlest emotions. It was capable of swelling into thunder peals, and then every ear tingled and every heart trembled." [1] Benjamin Franklin told how he doubted the reports he had heard about how 25,000 people heard George Whitefield preach without an amplifier for his tremendous voice. Franklin then gathered the facts as to how far Whitefield's voice could be heard, calculated the number of people who could be placed within an area thus covered, and came to the conclusion that the reports were true! Thirty thousand people could have heard Whitefield, according to Franklin's figures.

Another significant observation about Whitefield's delivery is the unusual intensity of feeling that he had as he preached. It was seldom that he preached a sermon without tears born of genuine soul passion appearing in his eyes. This was usual, not the unusual. Cornelius Winter, who accompanied him on many of his preaching journeys, said he hardly ever knew Whitefield to preach a sermon through to its finish without some tears. The intensity of his emotions was evident, not only in his feelings of pathos and passion, but also in the expression of other deep feelings as he spoke. The expression of his face would thrill an audience with its radiant joy, its solemn concern, its fear of judgment, and its expectancy of future bliss.

Whitefield's gestures were excellent as a help in expressing with his hand, his finger, or a movement of his arm

[1] Cincinnati: God's Revivalist Press, 1920, p. 483.

the "language" that made his words more vivid as he spoke them. His power of description was often so forceful that his audience was completely "carried away" during a moment of great feeling. James Lawson, in *Deeper Experiences of Famous Christians*, wrote that Lord Chesterfield was in the audience when Whitefield related an illustration about a poor, blind beggar stumbling dangerously along on a dark night near a steep cliff. Deserted by his dog near the edge of the precipice, he had nothing to aid him in his groping along the path but his staff. Lawson wrote:

> Whitefield was so warmed with his subject and enforced it with such graphic power that the whole audience was kept in breathless silence as if it saw the movements of the poor old man; and at length, when the beggar was about to take the fatal step which would have hurled him down the cliff to certain destruction, Lord Chesterfield actually made a rush forward to save him, exclaiming, "He is gone! He is gone!" [2]

After a study of George Whitefield's life and ministry, one writer aptly observed, "Few men, perhaps, ever gave their hearers so much wheat and so little chaff." The secret of Whitefield's "wheat-filled" sermons was his attitude toward his calling, his task, and his Lord. He loved souls for Christ's sake, and he loved men for their souls' sake. Some of his critics have said that his extemporaneous style of delivery reflected a carelessness in his study habits, but nothing could be further from the truth. He tried other styles; he studied longer hours and more extensively for this style than he would have been required to do for reading a manuscript or even memorizing a sermon. He preached as he preached because he believed he could achieve better results, and the facts verify that his opinion was a sound one.

Whitefield announced himself as in agreement with Luther's statement, "Study, meditation, and temptation are necessary for a minister of Christ." He also quoted many times the words of Bishop Sanderson: "Study without

[2] Fort Wayne, Ind.: Glad Tidings Publishing Company, 1911.

66

prayer is atheism, prayer without study is presumption." Whitefield, in the latter years of his ministry, read the complete six-volume work of Matthew Henry's expositions of the Scriptures—in a kneeling posture!

This man who "preached like a lion and looked like an angel" often said he would rather wear out than rust out. He got his wish. For thirty-four years he gave the best of his energy, his passion, his brain, his heart, and his strength, in spite of his frequent suffering from asthma. The crowd who heard him preach his last sermon in Newbury Port followed him home, where he stood on the stairs of the house, with a lighted candle, preaching on as though he had not already exhausted his strength. The candle died down, and he retired. It was his last sermon, and when he awoke, it was to behold the glory of the Christ he loved and served.

When John Wesley preached George Whitefield's funeral, the ministry of one of history's greatest evangelists was ended.

CHAPTER 11

John Fletcher

1729-85

"Pastors who pray for their flocks pray not in vain. Their fervent petitions are heard, sinners are converted, the faithful are edified."

These were the words of John W. Fletcher, Switzerland's gift to evangelical Protestantism, when he addressed a group of ministerial students in Wesley's England. He believed in the power of prayer, and his life was eloquent testimony to the fact that he was, above all other things, a man of prayer.

Born in Nyon, a town about fifteen miles from Geneva, on September 12, 1729, John Fletcher was a brilliant student and a lad of very tender and sensitive conscience in those early years of his life. Joseph Benson, Fletcher's biographer, tells of an incident which occurred soon after Fletcher went to England, which illustrates his sensitive conscience. Fletcher was employed as a tutor in Shropshire and was busy one Sunday evening composing music when a servant came in to make up his fire and rebuke him for his carelessness in so using the Sabbath. At first his pride was hurt and his resentment was aroused by such "impudence" on the part of a houseboy, but upon further reflection he felt the reproof was just. "He immediately put away the music," wrote Benson, "and from that hour became a strict observer of the Lord's day." [1]

Such strict honesty of mind and quick willingness to look objectively at his own conduct and motives characterized the soul of this spiritual warrior. Humility was his most prominent virtue, and prayer was his consuming passion.

Like his friend Wesley, John Fletcher did not find the peace his soul sought in any quick and easy way. He sought

[1] *The Life of the Rev. John W. De La Flechere* (New York: The Methodist Book Concern, 1914), p. 20.

earnestly for weeks that he might know his sins were forgiven, and many times he almost gave up seeking and surrendered to discouragement and despair. After a great amount of time spent in prayer and reading of God's word, however, he came to the realization that his sins were forgiven. Although his conversion came in a quiet manner and without great emotional accompaniment, he never doubted again that the witness was his.

John Fletcher was ordained to the ministry, according to Fisher, in 1755, and the same day helped John Wesley administer the sacrament of the Lord's Supper in the West Street Chapel. His first parish was in Madeley some time later, and God blessed his labor with unusual success. He not only ministered to the needs of his parishioners there, but preached in adjoining small towns about the countryside. One notices as he studies the lives of the pulpit giants of history that it can be said of all of them that they were perpetually busy in the work of winning men to Christ! The descriptive phrase which is so often used in speaking of Wesley—"He was out of breath in pursuit of souls"—might as well be said of Fletcher and all the others whom God used in the ministry of the message of full salvation and freedom from all sin.

Halford Luccock once remarked that "one of the priceless equipments of a preacher is a limp, of the sort that Jacob got from wrestling with an angel." John Fletcher must have had such a "limp," for he was a man of much prayer and deep devotion to God. Abel Stevens, writing a history of Methodism, said of Fletcher that he reflected the glory "of that Divine Presence with which he habitually lived in an intimacy and purity rarely if ever excelled by even the holiest men who have walked with God on earth."

John Fletcher prepared his sermons well. This fact may be due to his early formal education in Switzerland and to his habits of mental discipline, but at any rate he was never known to enter the pulpit poorly prepared. Most of his sermons were textual, and the average sermon had three or four main points which developed the thought with logic and clarity. He knew how to preach to the needs of his congregation. One is reminded in studying Fletcher's preaching of what W. E. Sangster said about capturing the interest of the hearers at the very beginning of the message. "However a man may start," Sangster declared, "let him make sure that his opening sentences have grappling irons; something cast out and taking firm hold of the minds of his hearers; something which will make them say to him in their hearts when he pauses: 'Go on! Go on!' " [2]

Fletcher's preaching was practical. Joseph Benson has quoted from one of his sermons the following practical advice for his listeners:

(1.) Get up early, and save time before you go to business, to put on the *whole armour of God,* by close meditation and earnest prayer.

(2.) Consider the temptation that most easily besets you, whether it be hurry, or vanity, or lightness, or want of recollection to do what you do as unto God. . . .

(3.) When your mind has been drawn aside, do not fret . . . but confess your fault, and calmly resume your former endeavour, but with more humility and watchfulness. [3]

His delivery was masterful in the pulpit. Gilpin is quoted as describing Fletcher's preaching in these words: "His subjects, his language, his gestures, the tone of his voice, and the turn of his countenance, all conspired to fix the attention and affect the heart. Without aiming at sublimity, he was truly sublime; and uncommonly eloquent without affecting the orator." [4]

He had as his design to convert, not captivate, his hearers, but he did both. He sought to secure their eternal salvation rather than their momentary applause, but they responded to his personal magnetism in accepting his zealous

[2] *The Craft of Sermon Construction* (Philadelphia: The Westminster Press, 1951), pp. 133-34.
[3] *Op cit.,* p. 89.
[4] *Ibid.,* pp. 76-77.

invitation that they know his exalted Lord. He was versatile in his delivery, using soft tones and soothing words when the occasion called for such, and using the thunder of Sinai's judgments to drive sin into the blazing light of scripture or cause "moneychangers" to quail before the power of the wrath of the Master's rebuking words.

John Fletcher preached holiness of heart and life, and he did so without compromise. Yet he presented the close and searching truth with kindness and with humility. Joseph Benson said of his preaching that it possessed the kind of humility which made him ready to acknowledge his own errors and also "induced him to throw the mantle of tender forbearance and forgiving love over those of others." To be uncompromising concerning the faults one may see in his own life and yet quick to believe the best when there is any question regarding the motives of another —this is one of the undeniable characteristics of the heart that is perfect in love toward God and toward his neighbor.

Phillips Brooks has aptly said: "The preacher must mainly rely upon the strength of what he does believe, and not upon the weakness of what he does not believe." John Fletcher believed what he preached, and his life indicates that he also practiced it.

It might be expected that a man of Fletcher's spirit would seldom cry out against sin or denounce evil in his preaching. But Fletcher was not only humble, he was also bold and courageous. He often raised his voice against Catholicism, which offered powerful opposition to the principles for which Fletcher and Wesley stood. After one such sermon, a Roman priest arose to call out to the audience as they left the building that he would answer Fletcher's argument later, and that there was no word of truth in Fletcher's message. Nothing more was ever heard from him, however, and no effect was seen resulting from his hysterical reply to John Fletcher's potent preaching.

His polemic ability is also seen in his preaching and writing against antinomianism, or the extreme form of

Calvinism which held that grace abolishes the law and all human effort. This is the heart of Fletcher's Arminianism.

The two-sided goal of the ideal sermon—that of having a divine message and yet also a human appeal—seems to have been accomplished in the preaching of John Fletcher. Luccock's wry observation that many sermons are like the miracle of Mohammed's coffin, suspended between heaven and earth, and actually touching neither, would not be true of Fletcher's sermons. He prayed until he believed he had a message from God's word; then he preached to people whom he knew and loved and understood. They felt he had been with God on the mount of blessing, but they were assured also that he now was with them in the valley of decision. Gilpin was right when he said of him, "This heavenly-minded servant of the Lord resembled his Master . . . in his love to precious souls." Like Christ, Fletcher had not only a vision of God's face but also an understanding of men's needs.

John Fletcher's highest goal, after pleasing the Christ he loved and served, was that he might be a brother to all Christians and that he might think of himself as their brother. He considered all the children of God as "members one of another," and he disdained to magnify the differences by which some parties of Christians have endeavored to separate themselves from each other. When the prayer of Jesus, as recorded in John 17, was answered in the heart of John Fletcher, it was completely answered. He not only felt the sanctifying power of the cleansing word, but he also knew the unifying power of the bond of perfect love shed abroad in the heart by the Holy Ghost: "that they all may be one; as thou, Father, art in me, and I in thee, that they also may be one in us."

Benson's greatest tribute to the man whose biography he presented to the readers of our generation was therefore given when he said of John Fletcher: "Sincere worshippers of every denomination, he regarded as *fellow citizens with the saints, and of the household of God:* desiring no greater honour than to be counted as their brother, and commanded as their servant." [5]

Such a man, and such a preacher, was John Fletcher, whose name is thoughtfully submitted to that illustrious list of names in the "hall of fame" for evangelical preachers.

[5] *Ibid.*, p. 313.

CHAPTER 12

Francis Asbury

1745-1816

It is no surprise that the words which appeared most often in the *Journal* of Francis Asbury were, "I preached." The first twenty-five years of his ministry he did nothing else but preach, for not until he was forty years old did he administer any of the ordinances of the church. En route to America from his native England he preached many times on shipboard. He preached on landing in Philadelphia, and thereafter for forty-five years scarcely a day passed that he did not preach. It has been estimated that he preached 17,000 sermons during his long and fruitful ministry.

Born near Birmingham in England in 1745, Francis Asbury never attended school after he was thirteen years of age. The reasons for this may be several; there were many hindrances in the way of a lad seeking his education in those days. One thing is certain, however, the reason had nothing to do with his own laziness, nor any lack of thirst for knowledge, as his later life testifies. Although this man did not attend school after his thirteenth year of life, he took Wesley's advice that he be a "man of one Book" and he learned his Bible thoroughly. After coming as a missionary to America he taught himself Greek and Hebrew, so that he could read his Bible in the original languages, and he also learned to read in Latin.

Francis Asbury was by nature a timid man, but an extremely conscientious one. George Mains, in his biography of Asbury, described the effect of his early home training as making him a "fearful, timid boy, morbidly introspective, fretting over religion and the likelihood of salvation." About his own youth he once said that he "neither dared an oath nor hazarded a lie, but was always prayerful and religious." He grew up in an atmosphere of fear lest he do something that might offend the awful, revengeful God about whom he had been taught.

The background of deep religious piety had its effect on his life and ministry. As bishop of the Methodist Church in America during those earliest days of its development here, he received the usual acclaim and its accompaniment of criticism. The "O'Kelly clash," when his plan of moving and stationing pastors came under severe criticism from some quarters, tried his faith and character but saw him emerge vindicated. That plan is still the custom in The Methodist Church, and one of his critics later said of him: "It may be said with absolute confidence that there was nothing in his career from the first, and nothing to which he gave his sanction, in the constitution of the church, that was tarnished by the slightest touch of self." [1]

Asbury was a man of prayer. On his knees before retiring, on his knees again on rising, after breakfast, dinner, supper, in pastoral calls, on all occasions, he prayed. His personal character and supreme devotion to God had their effect upon his ministry.

Francis Asbury's preaching was practical and evangelistic. He did not fear fanaticism, but he feared formalism. He once said, "Only the preaching that molds the lives of the people is great," and he always kept this principle before him in his own preaching. He preached for results. For him, style was incidental, culture was secondary, and any human considerations were important only in whatever measure they helped to achieve results.

William L. Duren wrote concerning Asbury's preaching: "He was plain, simple, and direct in his style, and he preached to the hearts of his hearers out of the heart of God." [2] A self-educated man, he was not as scholarly as some preachers, nor did he possess the imagination that

[1] Ezra Tipple, *Francis Asbury, the Prophet of the Long Road* (New York: The Methodist Book Concern, 1916), p. 266.

[2] *Francis Asbury* (New York: The Macmillan Company, 1928), p. 151. Used by permission of the author.

made some men's sermons sparkle and glitter. One who heard him thought his preaching "dignified and impressive"; and another said he was "systematic and dry." He himself professed that on some occasions he could not seem to express his thoughts "with readiness and perspicuity"; whereas, at other times, he continued, "proper sentences of Scripture and apt expressions occur without care or much thought." His preaching was not couched in placid phrases, the "empty stuff" which he feared, but was always an arraignment of sin and a call to live a life of holiness.

Asbury's preaching was to the conscience more than it was to the mind; yet he was well educated and fostered education. He did not strive for sensationalism, yet there was the sensationalism of stark reality in his message. One of his *Journal* accounts gives his own account of a sermon: "I delivered a close and awful discourse; I was very alarming. Seldom, if ever, have I felt more moved."

On occasions he swept his audiences with the mighty fervor that stirred him in his own soul. Ezra Tipple, another biographer, wrote of an incident in New England when the entire audience rose to its feet under the spell of Asbury's preaching. He sometimes indulged in a play of words, and he had a dry, keen sense of humor. He was usually serious, however, and before his audience had listened long, they too were serious.

Surprise was one of the best weapons Francis Asbury used in his preaching. He knew how sermons ought to be made, and he knew how they should be preached. His intimate knowledge of the Scriptures gave a sense of appropriateness to his texts. He never preached topical sermons, but always made his sermons the products of the texts from which he preached. Many preachers announce a text and immediately leave for some distant point, but when Asbury preached he announced a text and preached to it. With him proposition, argument, illustration, incident, and everything were either immediately drawn from or directly connected with his subject and his text.

His sermons abounded in scripture quotations, and his

phraseology was flavored with bits of sacred dialect and with numerous biblical illustrations. A study of his preaching reveals the influence of his devotion to the Bible upon his sermons.

In his *Journal* there are thousands of references to his sermons, but only about 700 of his texts are listed. Of these, some 170 are outlined.

It is interesting to observe that of these outlines given, eleven appear covering the period of 1771-86; eighty-seven from 1786-1800; and seventy-seven from 1801-15. Twelve of these texts have two outlines each, one has three, and the remainder one.

Forty-four of the sermons mentioned above are from Old Testament texts, sixteen of these being found in Isaiah and the Psalms. The New Testament contains 124 of these texts. Twenty-four of these are from the Gospels, eleven from the Acts, eighty-one from the Epistles, and four from Revelation.

He usually arose each morning between four and five o'clock to read his Bible and pray, and his messages reflected his rich saturation of soul with the word of God. He read it daily, not merely for sermon texts, but for spiritual illumination and soul food. It is little wonder that he could always be depended upon to preach from an appropriate text and to preach a practical message.

This man had little use for the elegant courtliness of the New England drawing room, but his mission was like the mission of John the Baptist, a voice crying in the wilderness. His preaching was extempore, and he frequently suffered lapses of memory, which were extremely embarrassing to him; but he was always practical, always fervently passionate, and always so simple that the most illiterate backwoodsman knew what he meant.

A survey of Francis Asbury's outlines reveals that he made no effort to appear profound. Most of his sermons were distinctly evangelistic in appeal. His sermon on the text, "Lord, are there few that are saved?" is:

I. What we are to be saved from.
II. How we are saved.
III. Why there are few.[3]

His outline for a sermon on repentance is:

I. The nature of repentance—the whole of religion.
II. The universality of repentance—all orders, stations, characters must repent.
III. The possibility of, and provision made for repentance—the gift of Christ—the death of Christ—the agency of the Spirit—the preaching of the Gospel—the means of grace.
IV. Necessity of repentance—from the consideration of the fall and our own actual transgressions, a future state and general judgment.
V. The time for repentance—*now*—this Gospel day of grace.[4]

His outlines show a majestic simplicity in exposition of the Scripture, a high order of spiritual comprehension and biblical insight, a deep devotion to Christ, and at times a tremendous oratorical style.

Jesse Lee said of him that he was "an excellent preacher"; Nathan Bangs, that he was "singularly imposing"; Joseph Travis, that he had a chaste and plain style; Joshua Marsden, that he was dignified, eloquent, and impressive. Bishop Fowler ranked Francis Asbury at the head of all Methodist preachers, and Schaff placed him among the eloquent preachers of America.

The words of George Rust pay tribute to one of the first great holiness preachers of America, when he said of Asbury:

He had the good humor of a gentleman, the eloquence of an orator, the fancy of a poet, the acuteness of a schoolman, the profoundness of a philosopher, the wisdom of a chancellor, the sagacity of a prophet, the reason of an angel, the piety of a saint. He had devotion enough for a cloister, learning enough for a university, and wit enough for a college virtuoso.[5]

[3] *Ibid.*, p. 141.
[4] *Ibid.*
[5] *Ibid.*, p. 95.

Although Rust's tribute seems a bit extravagant, there is no doubt that Francis Asbury was a mighty preacher of the word. He was a holiness preacher whose soul was aflame. Those who heard him saw the light and felt the heat in the impact of the Spirit's power upon him.

CHAPTER 13

Charles Simeon
1759-1836

"To humble the sinner, to exalt the Saviour, to promote holiness!"

Charles Simeon thus described the three great aims of his ministry, and such was the heart and soul of his message. For him, Christ was the center of all subjects for sinful men, and the gospel was the one remedy for their sin.

Born at Reading in 1759, Charles Simeon was sent as a boy of nine to Eton, and at nineteen he went with a scholarship to King's College, Cambridge. He succeeded there in due time to a fellowship, which he held until his death.

He served as a minister in the Church of the Holy Trinity in Cambridge for fifty-four eventful years. He knew the meaning of good reports and evil, the sound of favor and of opposition, the feeling of success and of failure. More than a century has passed since his death in 1836, and history's verdict is unmistakably one of favor on the results of the preaching of this passionate evangelist.

Simeon's labors in the pulpit were frequently characterized by the unusual. While substituting at old Cambridge for the regular minister, he captured the attention of this ordinarily conservative people and consistently and repeatedly filled the pews of the church. Such a thing was unheard of in those days. Not to be bound by the usual customs and traditions, he went about among the parishioners, from house to house, saying, "I am come to inquire after your welfare. Are you happy?" Such evident regard for their good disarmed them of their bitterness, and his success with them was no less than amazing.

The crowds that came to hear this "substitute" preach not only filled the pews but overflowed into the aisles and into the entrances. The vicar, Mr. Atkinson, whose good nature provides this delightful story, returned from his absence to be met with these words from his janitor, "O

Sir, I am so glad you are come; now we shall have some room!"

Charles Simeon represents Calvinism at its very best. He once related the substance of a conversation he had with John Wesley, and from his reactions, together with a notation in Wesley's diary which referred to the same meeting, it is evident that these two great saints saw eye to eye on many things. Certainly they were together on those things each thought to be of supreme importance.

John Wesley's *Journal* carries this notation:

> I went to Hinxworth [in Cambridgeshire], where I had the satisfaction of meeting Mr. Simeon, Fellow of King's College in Cambridge. He has spent some time with Mr. Fletcher, at Madelay, two kindred souls, much resembling each other in both fervor of spirit and in the earnestness of their address. He gave me the pleasing information that there are three parish churches in Cambridge wherein true scriptural religion is preached, and several young gentlemen who are happy partakers of it.[1]

Few men have held a more reverent attitude toward the word of God than did Charles Simeon. He was a thorough and constant student of the Scriptures and was an honest seeker after its plain meaning. He believed that the truths of revelation stood out clear and unmistakable in the Bible, and that that book was the sufficient treasure house of the Christian faith and the ultimate criterion in all matters of doctrine. He has never been accused of limiting its message in any private or particular way. He undoubtedly approached his study of the Scriptures with a mind and heart prepared to go all the way with its teaching, accepting the full implication of the words read in their own context. He refused to treat the Bible as a storehouse of proof-texts, where he could find corroboration for his own theories. He once expressed his attitude by saying: "My endeavor is to bring out of the Scriptures what is there, and not to trust in what I think might be there. I have a great jealousy on this head; never to speak more or less than I believe to be the mind of the Spirit in the passage I am expounding."

[1] December 20, 1784.

On controversy, Charles Simeon's words expressed his standing. He said:

I love the simplicity of the Scriptures, and I wish to receive and inculcate every truth precisely in the way, and to the extent, that it is set forth in the inspired Volume. Were this the habit of all divines, there would soon be an end of most of the controversies that have agitated and divided the Church of Christ.[2]

In doctrine he moved among the followers of Calvin, yet he appreciated the truth of Arminianism and shrank from the exaggerations of some of Calvin's adherents.

Carus described Charles Simeon as one whose delivery was "remarkably lively and impressive." He preached with an earnestness and with an intensity of fervor that was extraordinary in his day. Occasionally his gestures were almost grotesque from the earnestness of his feelings as he spoke, but his actions were genuine and unstudied and always sincere and serious.

Canon Abner Brown said of Simeon's preaching: "A single remark of Wilberforce's in reference to a specific occasion accurately describes him at all times; 'Simeon is in earnest.' One could hardly help noticing a peculiar look of earnest reality at all times stamped upon his countenance." [3]

His hearers usually were satisfied that he deeply felt what he was saying and meant every word of it to the fullest possible extent. His mannerisms and gestures, peculiar at times, were forgotten as those in his audience listened with breathless attention as to an ambassador from God delivering a powerful and loving message to each one of them individually.

Simeon's language was accurate and strong. His distinct articulation, unlabored utterance, accurate pronunciation, and frequent eloquence of style fixed the hearer's attention upon the message and not on the speaker. Moule, his biographer, said of his literary style that it was "a good specimen

[2] Handley C. G. Moule, *Charles Simeon* (London: The Inter-Varsity Fellowship, 1948).
[3] *Ibid.* p. 72.

of the writing of the closing eighteenth century, when our prose attained a high general standard."

Simplicity without tameness, eloquence without ornamentation, passion and earnestness without affectation—a difficult goal for any speaker to achieve, but excellently practiced by Simeon, according to those who heard him preach. His objectives were to be understood, to come close to the conscience and heart, and to produce action.

In his sermon "The Excellency and Glory of the Gospel," from the text in Eph. 3:19, "that ye might be filled with all the fulness of God," he began with the words:

In my text it is said that a view of this sublime mystery will "fill us with all the fulness of God." And what can be meant by this? Can it be supposed that a creature can ever resemble God in his *natural* perfection? No, but in His *moral* perfections we both may and must resemble Him, if ever we would behold the face of God in peace.[4]

He continued his introduction of his message by explaining:

In a word, we should resemble God who is Light itself. In light, you know, there is an assemblage of widely different rays; some of which, if taken separately, might be thought to approximate rather to darkness than to light. But if the more brilliant rays were taken alone, though they might produce a glare, they would never make a light. It is the union of all in their due proportion and in simultaneous motion that constitutes light; and then only when all the graces are in simultaneous exercise, each softening and tempering its opposite, then only, I say, do we properly resemble God.[5]

Abner Brown recalled having heard one of Simeon's sermons which seemed unusually forceful. He described the preacher's illustration of the keeper of a lighthouse on an island in the Firth of Forth. Simeon supposed the keeper to have let the lights go out, according to Brown,

and in the consequence the coast was strewed with wrecks and with dead and mangled bodies; and that the wailings of widows

[4] *Ibid.* p. 73.
[5] *Ibid.*

and orphans were everywhere heard. He supposed the delinquent brought out for examination before a full court and an assembled people; and at last the answer to be given by him, that he was "asleep"—"*Asleep!*" The way in which he made his "asleep" burst on the ears of his audience, who were hanging in perfect stillness on his lips, contrasting the cause with the effects, I remember to this day.[6]

Once after preaching a sermon on the eternal covenant, he vigorously interrupted the instrumental postlude with the exclamation, "No music! Let the people retire in silence and think upon the covenant!" To Charles Simeon, the work of the pulpit was inexpressibly important, and he did not attempt to conceal his feelings concerning this.

On another occasion, in Scotland, when "God had been much with him" as he preached, the minister of the church, just after the sermon, in the vestry, began to ask him about his travels. "Speak to me of heaven, Sir," he answered, "and I can talk with you, but do not speak to me about earth at this moment, for I cannot talk about it."

Simeon's preaching was soul-moving. It has been said that no sermon is what a sermon should be if it is not also an action. Simeon's sermons were actions. They appealed to the poor and the unlearned as well as to the educated minds of Cambridge's scholars.

Simeon's lectures on preaching reveal his understanding of the art he so capably developed in his own ministry. He saw that the sermon must have unity of theme and message, that it must be intelligible, and that it must be interesting. Charles Haddon Spurgeon often said that the "pastor who would keep his church full must first preach the Gospel, and then preach it with three adverbs in mind—earnestly, interestingly, fully." In substance, this seemed to be Simeon's prescription also, for he certainly made it his practice.

He believed the minister of the Word must not becloud his text, but "let it speak." He advised his young friends to know both what they meant to say and how to say it so as to arrest and to reward attention. He reminded them

[6] *Ibid.* p. 74.

that a pastoral sermon should not be a teatise out of place or an oration developed from the mere starting point of a text, but rather "a setting forth of God's Word by a commissioned messenger in an assembly of living men." He insisted upon care in exposition, clearness of arrangement, and directness of appeal. As to the actual delivery, he advised them to prepare their material fully and carefully, but to leave the wording of it to the moment of delivery.

The traditions of English preaching had long been curiously artificial. The sermon was either read from a manuscript or committed to memory and recited. There was a pulpit manner and voice quite different from that of the preacher's common life. It had come to be thought that a natural earnestness was entirely out of place in the pulpit. Charles Simeon, in advising a natural, extemporaneous delivery and a conversational tone, revitalized the revolutionized English preaching among those who followed his pattern.

He recorded one incident that portrays the inner feeling and utter religious devotion of a saintly preacher under persecution. He said:

When I was an object of much contempt and derision I strolled forth one day, buffeted and afflicted, with my little Testament in my hand. I prayed earnestly to my God that He would comfort me with some cordial from His Word, and that, on opening the book, I might find some text which should sustain me. . . . The first text which caught my eye was this: *"They found a man of Cyrene, Simon by name; him they compelled to bear His cross."* You know Simon is the same name as Simeon. What a word of instruction was here—what a blessed hint for my encouragement! To have the cross laid upon me, that I might bear it for Jesus—what a privilege! It was enough. Now I could leap and sing for joy as one whom Jesus was honoring with a participation of His sufferings.[7]

Such a spirit and attitude offers the best explanation for the effect of Charles Simeon's preaching upon those who heard him.

[7] *Ibid.* pp. 59-60.

CHAPTER 14

Peter Cartwright

1785-1872

It seemed that in his day, a Methodist preacher feeling his call to preach, did not hunt up a college or a Biblical institute, but rather he hunted up a horse, and some traveling apparatus, and with his library of Bible, hymnbook, and Discipline, he would start out with a text that never wore out, or grew stale, "Behold the Lamb of God that taketh away the sin of the world!"

Thus wrote Clarence Edward Macartney in his book *Sons of Thunder, Pulpit Powers of the Past*.[1] The man he is describing is Peter Cartwright—rough, muscular, courageous, and crude, but at the same time gentle, kind, humble, and considerate toward the men and women to whom he preached.

Cartwright was born in Virginia in 1785 but moved to Kentucky when he was six years old. His mother, a consecrated, sanctified Methodist, surrounded him with her love and prayers during those early days of his life. But Peter followed in the steps of his wicked father. He writes of those early years, as quoted by J. G. Lawson, in *Deeper Experiences of Famous Christians:*

I was naturally a wild, wicked boy, and delighted in horse-racing, card-playing, and dancing. My father restrained me little, though my mother often talked to me, wept over me, and prayed for me, often drew tears from my eyes; and though I often wept under preaching and resolved to do better and seek religion, yet I broke my vows, went into bad company, rode races, played cards, and danced.[2]

At sixteen he was so strongly convicted of sin that he thought he would die. With his mother's help he prayed until peace came, and it was three months later in one of

[1] Westwood, N. J.: Fleming H. Revell Company, 1929, p. 157.
[2] Anderson, Ind.: The Warner Press, 1911, p. 230.

the many Methodist camp meetings of that day that he was gloriously converted. He joined the Methodist Church immediately and was called to preach very soon afterwards. His first sermon, preached in Logan County, Kentucky, was from the text in Isa. 26:4, "Trust ye in the Lord for ever: for in the Lord Jehovah is everlasting strength."

"The Lord gave light, liberty, and power," Cartwright said of that service, "and the congregation was melted in tears." Among the converts who knelt at the altar that night was a professed infidel, who was genuinely converted and later joined the church.

Broad shoulders, a massive head, black, piercing eyes, and clear, heavy voice made Peter Cartwright a welcome friend and a dreaded enemy in the conflict between sin and holiness. Unorthodox but effective, he possessed the common sense which helped compensate for his lack of formal education, and what he didn't know was overlooked in the midst of an extravagant portion of enthusiasm in his spirit-filled ministry.

William Warren Sweet observed that Cartwright's personality fit into the Western frontier so well that his success can easily be understood. "The great mass of our western people," he wrote, "wanted a preacher that could mount a stump, a block, or old log, or stand in the bed of a wagon, and without note or manuscript, quote, expound, and apply the word of God to the hearts and consciences of the people." [3] Such a man was Peter Cartwright. It has been said that his circuits were like "lines of battle," and they were continuously in a state of excitement, if not outright commotion!

"Muscular evangelism" was the term one writer used in describing Cartwright's ministry, and it is true that this early Methodist firebrand was known throughout the Cumberland Mountains as one of that section's best fighters. Strange as it seems in the light of present-day niceties, in

[3] *Religion on the American Frontier*, Vol. IV: *The Methodists* (Chicago: University of Chicago Press, 1946).

his day Cartwright saw nothing inconsistent in a good
Christian thrashing of rowdies who sought to disturb his
meetings—"so long as it was done in a spirit of love," he
would explain. On more than a few occasions unruly attend-
ants were literally thrown out of the meetings they sought
to disturb, and then Cartwright would continue his sermons.

Afraid of no one, Peter Cartwright must have inspired
interest if not awe as he conducted his tent revivals and
camp meetings. In his autobiography, edited by W. P. Strickland, Cartwright tells of two finely dressed young ladies
who came to his meeting, attended by their two brothers.
The ladies came down to the front, but the boys stood by the
door. Cartwright was not feeling very well, so he took some
peppermint from his pocket and put it into his mouth. Just
as he did, the young ladies "took the jerks"—a common
emotional phenomenon in those times—and the brothers
became enraged. They said they had seen the preacher take
something from his pocket, and they accused him of causing
the condition the girls were now displaying. They threatened
to give the evangelist a good beating. Cartwright took advantage of their accusation and, reaching into his pocket,
said, "I gave your sisters the jerks, and now I'm going to
give them to you." The boys fled immediately, but later the
same boys and their two sisters were all converted and
joined the church.

Unorthodox, unique, and unusual are not strong enough
words to adequately describe Peter Cartwright in action.
On one occasion when he stopped for a night's lodging in
a home in the Cumberland Mountains, the people were having a dance. A young lady courteously asked Peter to dance,
and for a moment he was speechless, but then he thought of
a plan. He described what followed:

I rose as gracefully as I could; I will not say with some emotion
but with many emotions. The young lady moved to my right side;
I grasped her right hand with my right hand, while she leaned
her left arm on mine. In this position we walked on the floor.
The whole company seemed pleased at the act of politeness in
the young lady shown to a stranger. I spoke to the fiddler to hold

a moment, and added that for several years I had not undertaken any matter of importance without first asking the blessing of God upon it, and I desired now to ask the blessing of God upon this beautiful young lady and the whole company.[4]

Cartwright goes on to describe the consternation which at first seized his partner while he knelt there to pray, holding firmly to her hand so that she could not flee, and how she finally knelt with him, as did perhaps thirty or more others in the room. Some prayed while others fled into other rooms of the house and into the yard. The dance never did get under way that night! Cartwright prayed and exhorted, and as a result a "society" was organized with thirty-two members.

With such rough and ready tactics as he displayed, he is considered by some to be unworthy of the respect due a minister. But there is another side to the man. He was keen and sharp in debate—on one occasion he had a verbal encounter with Joseph Smith of the Mormons, and Smith came off second best according to those who were present. It is not too widely known that Peter Cartwright served two terms in the Illinois legislature, and sought the nomination of his party for a seat in the Congress. The opponent who defeated him was Abraham Lincoln.

Quick wit came to his rescue when a lack of education hindered him. Once a learned minister tried to bring contempt on Cartwright's ignorance by addressing him in Greek. Cartwright, of course, did not understand a word of it, but he was not to be outdone. He replied in German, which he had learned as a child from a neighbor. The minister thought it was Hebrew and was amazed. He told Cartwright he was the first educated Methodist preacher he had ever seen!

Since none of his sermons is published, we know only that his themes were mostly on Christ, the power of God, and the punishment of hell. His sermons were largely topical in construction. He preached at least forty-five minutes, and

[4] Peter Cartwright, *Autobiography of Peter Cartwright*, Ed. W. P. Strickland (New York: Carlton & Porter, 1857), p. 237.

many times an hour and a half. His gestures were frequent and vigorous. As many as twenty thousand heard him without the aid of amplifiers. Emotion was strong in the pulpit and in the audience when Peter Cartwright preached. Men and women "fell" under the power of the conviction that came upon his hearers as the word went forth. He possessed wit and grace, mirth and dignity. He wrote a characteristic summary of his meetings in his auto-biography: "We had some very powerful displays of Divine grace, and a goodly number obtained religion, and I received about seventy into society, appointed leaders, met classes, sung, prayed, and exhorted, and under the circumstances, did the best I knew how."

He died at the age of eighty-seven, after fifty-three years of preaching, during which time he preached 14,600 times. During the first twenty years he often preached twice a day and sometimes three times, and during the latter years an average of four times a week. One writer observed: "We may see some of his methods as crude, but we can never criticize his motives. He preached with a heart of love, and even when he was a little rough with the rowdies, they knew he loved them." [5]

Rough and hardy as an oak; overflowing with geniality and humor; a tireless worker and a traveler; a sagacious counselor, giving often in the strangest disguises of wit and humor the shrewdest suggestions of wisdom—Peter Cartwright is an example of one of the most noted, most unique, and most interesting evangelists in the history of the pioneer West.

---

[5] Eugene Simpson, "The Life and Ministry of Peter Cartwright," (Unpublished paper, Nazarene Theological Seminary).

CHAPTER 15

Charles G. Finney

1792-1875

> As I turned and was about to take
> a seat by the fire, I received a mighty
baptism with the Holy Ghost. Without any expectation of it,
without ever having the thought in mind that there was any such
thing for me, without any recollection that I had ever heard the
thing mentioned by any person in the world, the Holy Spirit
descended upon me in a manner that seemed to go through me
body and soul!

Thus wrote Charles G. Finney in his *Memoirs* concerning
the religious experience that gave power to his ministry and
victory in his personal life.[1] From the day of that experience
until the day of his death, this devoted preacher pressed the
claims of the gospel upon those who heard him, and the results of his ministry demand that his name be placed among
those who have earned for themselves the title of "evangelist."

Born of nonreligious parents in Warren, Connecticut, in
1792, Charles Grandison Finney had very little in his home
environment that would help make him the preacher he later
became. His family, hardy pioneers, moved westward into
the relatively unbroken wilderness of middle New York
state when he was yet a lad. These New England settlers
possessed very few religious books, but they immediately
established schools. They seemed to appreciate the value of
education, but had no idea of the importance of religious
training. Finney himself wrote later that there was "very
little intelligent preaching of the gospel" during his impres-
sionable years as a boy, and that neither of his parents made
any profession of religion. Finney's home offered little
chance for spiritual awakening. His early life was typically
what might be termed today "secularized." He was taught
the necessity of hard work, the rudiments of basic knowl-

[1] New York: A. S. Barnes & Company, 1876.

edge, the value of thriftiness, frugality, and honesty; but he was not introduced to the Christ, whose life and teaching are examples of all these qualities.

The education Charles G. Finney pursued would not be considered above the ordinary by present-day standards but certainly must have been better than most men received in his time. The wilderness schools were barely adequate for the development of such skills as reading, writing, and arithmetic, but Charles had the ambition to go to New England for his high school education and put himself through by teaching in the elementary schools as his means of livelihood. After completing high school he joined the law office of Squire Wright Adams and studied law.

It was during the time that he studied law that Finney discovered for the first time, apparently, the importance of the Bible. He wrote in his *Memoirs:*

I found the old authors frequently quoting the scriptures, and referring especially to the Mosaic institutes, as authority for many of the principles of common law. This excited my curiosity so much that I went and purchased a Bible, the first I had ever owned; whenever I found a reference by the law authors to the Bible, I turned to the passage and consulted it in its connection. This soon led to my taking a new interest in the Bible, and I read and meditated on it much more than I had ever done before in my life.[2]

Thus his study of law had a distinct influence on the preaching of Charles G. Finney. Through law, he learned to appreciate and later to love the Bible, from which flows the source of all that is orderly and just and right. From law he learned also the importance of straight thinking and clear, logical presentation of thought. Most important, from the interest awakened in the Scriptures through the study of law, Finney became more interested in religion and the church.

The young lawyer's conversion was delayed, and almost prevented completely, by his difficulty in understanding why

[2] *Op cit.*

the Christian people he observed—and sinners under conviction do look at the Christians very closely—prayed so much but did not receive the answers to their prayers very often. The Holy Spirit was faithful to guide him into an understanding of the truth, however, and he decided as he studied the Word, that their prayers were not answered because they had not met the conditions. It was in a wooded grove on the way to his work that he turned aside to settle his commitment to God. While at first he could not seem to get his prayers through because he was fearful lest someone might hear him pray, he soon became so overwhelmed with his sense of wickedness that he cried at the top of his voice that, as he described it, "I would not leave that place if all the men on earth and all the devils in hell surrounded me." Needless to add, the Spirit gave him the promise and peace came. Thank God, whether it is an old-fashioned altar in an evangelistic holiness church, or out in the woods where a spiritually ignorant lawyer seeks forgiveness, God's grace is sufficient.

With a genuine conversion, and later an experience of the Spirit's baptism such as that described in the beginning of this chapter, it is no wonder that Charles G. Finney willingly answered God's call to preach the gospel and that his preaching provided the persuasive power that brought a half million souls to Christ and salvation.

Finney's theological training came by way of self-study, since his formal education was designed to prepare him for the practice of law. He read widely, and his formal preparation qualified him for the position of president of Oberlin College, which he held for fifteen fruitful years from 1851 until 1866. It was here that Finney became identified with the theological position known as the Oberlin theology, which vigorously opposed the extreme Calvinism which seemed to stress the sovereignty of God by neglecting the free will of man. Finney and the Oberlin evangelists seemed to stress free will by modifying the sovereignty of God.

Finney's preparation for preaching combined together the qualities of sane, clear, thorough scholarship with consuming soul passion. He demonstrates the truism that although no great preacher must be highly educated, every great preacher must be possessed with a desire to apply himself to the best possible performance of his task.

Raymond Edman, writing in *Finney Lives On,* sees in the preaching of Charles G. Finney a certain homeliness that might mistakenly be seen as coarseness.[3] Some of his critics accused him of being "colloquial." He was not conformed to the formal, rigid pattern of "dignity" that prevailed in his day. His style was deliberately and designedly plain-spoken. He spoke the language his hearers could understand.

Finney had the ability to preach the rugged truth in condemnation of sin and wickedness in such a manner as to cause sinners to tremble with conviction, yet with a spirit of tenderness and love such as caused sinners to weep for their wickedness and want to hear more from this man of God. A. M. Hills was so impressed with this quality in Finney's preaching that he declared: "Would to God that all of us who are called to preach would learn this simple lesson from this great preacher's experience! The way to preach these stern truths and the judgments of God is with weeping eyes and a compassionate heart." [4]

Herbert L. Rogers observed in his study of Finney's ministry a unique power that came through prayer. Perhaps his social life helped him preach so as to rebuke sin, yet with a spirit of compassion which the sinner could not overlook. Prayer bands were organized wherever Finney held revivals, and a saintly character known as Father Nash dedicated himself to the ministry of prayer in Finney's campaigns—praying while Finney preached—so that there can be no doubt as to the place of prayer in Finney's success as an evangelist.

Finney's sermons are not by any stretch of the imagination models of homiletical excellence. His introductions

[3] Westwood, N. J.: Fleming H. Revell Company, 1951.
[4] *Life of Charles G. Finney* (Cincinnati: Office of God's Revivalist, 1902).

were usually interesting and arresting, but his sermon body often resembled a lawyer's brief more than a sermon outline. For example, in his sermon "The Religion of Public Opinion," the "outline" consists of twenty points at which professing Christians either measure up or fail. The reader can take his choice: Is this a twenty-point sermon, or—of all things—a "one-pointer" with twenty subpoints? His sermon on "Prevailing Prayer" is a topical development of the proposition that "there are two kinds of means requisite to promote a revival; one is to influence men, the other to influence God." His two main divisions deal with two thoughts in his proposition, personal work and prayer.

His conclusions were often a series of "remarks" by which the central thought of the message was emphasized. His illustrations were largely from everyday experience and life situations and were a very significant part in the effectiveness of his preaching.

Finney's appearance was stately and imposing. He was six feet tall and used enough gestures to add force to his words, but never enough to detract from them. Hills writes that "he was entirely free from mannerism" and that his intonation and emphasis were "perfect." Edman, his biographer, was impressed with Finney's appearance. He wrote: "He spoke with directness and depth of feeling, with great searching eyes that seemed to peer into the very innermost depths of his hearers." [5]

It was customary in Finney's time for preachers to prepare oratorical messages which could be read from the manuscript, but he disliked this method keenly. He was a strong believer in the extemporaneous method of delivery, and he not only used this method, but urged his pupils in Oberlin to follow it.

What one quality, more than any other, made Charles G. Finney the great evangelist he was? Perhaps the answer to this question must be that there were two qualities in his life and ministry which are really one, for they are in-

[5] *Op cit.*

separable. He relied upon prayer, and with his utter dependence upon prayer he relied upon personal work. The latter was begun immediately after his own conversion, when, Basil Miller points out, within twenty-four hours after he found Christ he had won several converts, among them a lawyer and a distiller.

The theologian Charles Hodge was impressed with Finney's "relentless logic." Henry Ward Beecher admired the masterful way he conducted his meetings. But when Charles G. Finney learned to wait upon God until the Holy Spirit came to direct and to empower, he found the secret of successful soul winning.

CHAPTER 16

Henry Ward Beecher

1813-87

"I remember that flock which I found gathered in the wilderness consisted of twenty persons. Nineteen of them were women, and the other was nothing. I remember the days of our poverty, our straightness. I was sexton of my own church at that time." [1]

This is not the life story of a home missionary pastor whose years were spent hewing out a kingdom where the gospel of full salvation is preached; it is the reminiscence of a man who for forty years was pastor of the Plymouth Congregational Church in Brooklyn, and after the first two years received an annual salary equal to that of the mayor of the city—$20,000. This is the way he started, as so many great preachers have begun their ministry, in the close community of a small but sympathetic congregation. This is the story of Henry Ward Beecher.

The first struggling attempt at pastoral ministry for Beecher occurred some twenty miles west of Cincinnati in a village named Lawrenceburg, Indiana. His next charge, in Indianapolis, was more fruitful and rewarding and was followed by his outstanding pastorate in Brooklyn, where he became known as one of the unique preachers of his day. Lewis O. Brastow in his book *Representative Modern Preachers* wrote of him that "by most he has been estimated as superior in popular effectiveness to all other American preachers of whatever period, and by not a few as the greatest pulpit orator of the Christian church." [2]

[1] Lyman Abbott, *Henry Ward Beecher* (Boston: Houghton Mifflin Company, 1903), p. 47.

[2] New York: The Macmillan Company, 1904, p. 105.

Henry Ward Beecher was born in Litchfield, Connecticut, on June 24, 1813, into the home of one of the foremost preachers, reformers, Calvinists, and controversalists of his day—the Rev. Lyman Beecher. Speaking of this home, the cynical Robert G. Ingersoll has charged in one of his diatribes as quoted by Paxton Hibben:

> Henry Ward Beecher was born in a Puritan penitentiary, of which his father was one of the wardens—a prison with very narrow and closely-grated windows. . . . In this prison the creed and catechism were primers for children, and from a pure sense of duty their loving hearts were stained and scarred with the religion of John Calvin.[3]

A truer picture of Beecher's home is seen in the words of Hibben:

> His house was the rallying place of those who opposed the loosening of the strait ties of Calvinism upon the spirit and the constricting bonds of puritanism upon the behavior. Armed with the twin weapons wielded by the clergy of his day—education and the terror of divine wrath—Lyman Beecher and his fellows were conservative because it was simpler to compel men to fit their spirits into the mold of rigid dogma than to write a theological prescription that will meet the needs of mankind.[4]

Beecher's own recollections of his early life paint a picture of a father who was above all a good man. Henry is quoted in his son's book, *A Biography of Rev. Henry Ward Beecher*, as saying that his father never once set a poor example before him. "I remember particularly," Henry said, "that I never heard from him a word of uncharitableness, nor saw a symptom of envy or jealousy." [5] As for his mother, who died when he was a child, she left an indelible impression upon his life. Joseph Howard, in *Life of Henry Ward Beecher*, points out that "her face, her temper, her goodness, along every line of family development, were con-

[3] *Henry Ward Beecher: An American Portrait* (New York: The Press of Reader's Club, 1942), p. 3.
[4] *Ibid.*, p. 3.
[5] New York: C. L. Webster Company 1888, p. 17.

stantly used as illustrations in his writings and his sermons." [6]

One thing must be said in behalf of Lyman Beecher's wisdom in dealing with his son Henry. Had he used less tact and patience, his illustrious son might never have entered the ministry. For young Henry had his mind set on a career at sea and was intent on joining the navy. Long before most of the child and adolescent psychology books were published, the astute father talked this matter over with his son. He assured him if he wanted to be a sailor, not just the common, ordinary sailor, but an officer, he must study mathematics, navigation, and many other such subjects. The lad agreed, and off he went to school at the age of fourteen. It was while he was engaged in his studies at Mount Pleasant that a great religious revival broke out, and Henry was converted. His biographer son points out that never once afterward was anything said about his going to sea. From that time forward his goal was the ministry of the gospel of Jesus Christ.

Graduated from Amherst College, Henry entered Lane Seminary in Cincinnati, where his father, Lyman Beecher, was president of the seminary and professor of theology. While here he experienced an even more satisfying religious awakening. Lyman Abbott comments that "from the time of that revelation he seemed never to have had a doubt respecting his mission, or a hesitancy about endeavoring to fulfil it, only hesitancy about the path to be taken towards its fulfilment."

What was there about the preaching of this man who at the age of thirty-four began a forty-year pastorate in one of the most influential pulpits of America and became known as one of America's great pastoral preachers?

The influence of a great preacher-father, the lasting effects of a wholesome, religious early home life, the natural endowments of a gifted personality, the normal results of a thorough and adequate training and preparation for his

[6] Philadelphia: Hubbard Brothers Publishers, 1887, p. 30.

work—all these without question played their part. But more specifically, and more significantly, there were other factors. A study of his methods reveals some of these.

Henry Ward Beecher loved and understood people. His close contact with them had its effect upon his preaching style and made his ministry effective. The study of men seemed important to him, according to Lyman Abbott, who wrote that "it was partly this study of people who so molded his preaching and gave him his vivid imagination . . . and dramatic personification of every character he wished to portray."

Examples of this style of dramatic personification can be seen in his sermons. In "The Courtesy of Conscience" (I Cor. 10:28-29: "Conscience, I say, not thine own, but of the other: for why is my liberty judged of another man's conscience?") he speaks of certain church people who murder the king's English, sing cantering hymns, and "shout out their prayers from catapults." In this sermon he likens the dogmatic conscience to "the bulldog who rushes out and sits down on the doctrine and everybody is judged by it." In his sermon "The God of Comfort," such phrases as "God's love letters written in dark ink," and, "You were gold in the rock, and God played the miner, and blasted you out of the rock!" are expressions his listeners can feel as well as understand.

His graphic language sometimes brought criticism as well as admiration. He was accused by Sinclair Lewis of being sensational. Lewis wrote: "He was a powerful writer of trash, and all over the land, families got out the carry-all to drive to town and hear him speak on everything from 'The Strange Women' to the cozy theory that a worker who did not rejoice in bringing up five children on a wage of a dollar a day was a drunken gunny-sack." [7] But Lewis' harsh words serve only to emphasize a quality in the message and content of Henry Ward Beecher's preaching that was practical, down-to-earth, and vivid. He spoke to people's needs, and he loved and understood them with their problems.

[7] Paxton Hibben, *op. cit.*, p. vii.

Add to the factors of natural gifts, adequate training, deep religious experience, devotion to Christ, and this unusual love for the understanding of humankind in their everyday problems of life, another significant factor in the success of Henry Ward Beecher as a pastoral preacher. He possessed an unusual dramatic gift and did not hesitate to make use of it. He appealed to the emotions equally as well as to the intellect and to the will.

Robert Crew expresses this in his summary of Beecher's preaching style:

He used his imagination, his feeling, his sympathy, as the organ of religious knowledge. Beecher could describe with singular exactness the movements and speech of a drunkard, or a blacksmith, or a fisherman, or a farmer. He could change his voice and delivery to suit the content, from a quiet, gentle tone to the most penetrating severity. His eyes would flash fire and his cheeks would glow red, or his eyes would fill with tears and his audience would weep copiously with him when his feelings changed.[8]

Henry Ward Beecher used illustrations freely and expertly. There are at least seven full-length illustrations in addition to some metaphors and analogies in "Conflicts of the Christian Life." In this same sermon he quotes twenty-six times from the Bible—seven from the Old and nineteen from the New Testament.

He preached with notes, but was at his best when, under the inspiring influence of his audience, he let his thoughts come to him as he went along. More evangelistic than doctrinal in his emphasis, he always used the extemporaneous style of delivery.

Beecher was more liberal in his theology than many of the American preachers of his time. He broke away from the rigid Calvinism he inherited, and his preaching typified a whole trend in preaching in his day.

An outstanding contribution to his times was his heroic leadership in the slavery controversy and in the preserva-

[8] "Beecher's Life and Ministry" (Unpublished paper, Nazarene Theological Seminary).

tion of the Union. These and other important social issues were treated vigorously in his pulpit. It must be added that his establishment of the Lyman Beecher lectureship on preaching at Yale in honor of his father is one of the most important contributions to the art of preaching of all time.

Edna Dean Proctor and A. Moore compiled from their notes on Beecher's sermons some of his thoughts, and they preserved the following as one of the statements which was very characteristic of his preaching:

> The most you can do to a good man is to persecute him; and the worst that persecution can do is to kill him. And killing a good man is as bad as it would be to spite a ship by launching it. The soul is built for heaven, and the ship for the ocean, and blessed be the hour that gives both to the true element.[9]

Henry Ward Beecher practiced this way of life. Persecuted viciously by his enemies—even involved in a moral scandal, which was of course never proved—he maintained his faith in God and his boundless love for people, and he left an example of preaching ministry which every pastor may well follow.

[9] *Life Thoughts* (Glasgow and London: Wm. Collins Sons & Company, 1867), p. 1.

CHAPTER 17

Frederick W. Robertson
1816-53

"You preach positively instead of negatively, you state truths which they cannot deny; . . . you set up your truth and they are dismayed to find, if that be true, their view is knocked down, but you did not knock it down." [1]

This was the tribute F. W. Robertson's physician paid him when in the course of the conversation the subject of his attitude toward those who disagreed with his preaching came into discussion. The good doctor described his pastor better than he realized. Gentle but firm, kind but unswerving, independent and nonconforming, yet keenly aware of others and their feelings, Frederick W. Robertson was a brilliant Bible expositor and outstanding example of pastoral preacher.

Born in London on February 3, 1816, he lived only thirty-seven years before his death at Brighton in August, 1853. The intensity of his spirit, the burning passion of his heart, the driving pace he demanded of himself, and the overwhelming burden he carried for his work all took their toll in a life that blazed brilliantly and burned out in so few years, yet left an example of courage and eloquence for every minister to follow.

A high-spirited boy, young Frederick wanted more than anything else to be a soldier. James R. Blackwood, in *The Soul of Frederick W. Robertson,* writes of his dream of military life, with its heroic glory and world travel: "He loved the rattle of officers' swords and the clink of spurs, but more than these, the table talk of soldiers, barracks incidents, campaigns fought again on winter evenings before the fire, and rumors that traveled fast when soldiers met. His ears were tuned to martial strains." [2]

[1] James R. Blackwood, *The Soul of Frederick W. Robertson* (New York: Harper & Brothers, 1947), p. 104.
[2] *Ibid.*, p. 5.

It was in his twentieth year that he yielded to his father's wish, abandoned the idea of a military career, and entered Oxford University to prepare himself for the ministry. None of his biographers have much to say about his call to preach. It would seem that he accepted the idea of devoting his life to preaching primarily because of the need as he saw it, in the logical and analytical way he approached all of life's decisions. It seemed the right thing to do, and he did it. It was as simple as that.

He was graduated at the top of his class at Oxford, and ordained a minister in the Anglican church in 1840. After seven years of pastoral service in Oxford and Cheltenham, he began his ministry in Trinity Chapel in Brighton, where he won acclaim for "his earnestness, his eloquence, and his lucid explanation of the reasonableness of spiritual truth."

Lewis O. Brastow, in *Representative Modern Preachers,* observed that "it will always be an honor to the Anglican church that it was the spiritual home of Frederick Robertson." He immediately points out, however, that the Anglicans cannot claim him in the broader sense, for Robertson "was the product of a broader world than that in which his church moves." [3] He was loyal yet independent, if one can imagine such a paradoxical situation. He was never bound by conventionalism nor a slave to institutionalism, yet none could accuse him of being heretical or disloyal. Perhaps his early life had its effect on his ministry. Stopford A. Brooke wrote, in *The Life, Letters, and Lectures of F. W. Robertson,* that the Brightonians of his day had a distinctive flair for argument and "were always sniffing the air to catch the scent of the heretic." [4] Such an atmosphere would stimulate independent thinking in a brilliant young mind.

Robertson's method of dealing with argumentative fellow ministers is described by Brooke, who quoted him as having remarked: "It is an endless task to be refuting error. Plant

[3] *Op. cit.,* p. 49.
[4] New York: Harper & Brothers, 1903, p. 123.

truth, and the errors will pine away." [5] Thus his preaching had a distinctive tone of authority. He prepared carefully and thoroughly, until he knew he was correct in his understanding of his scripture; then he spoke decisively. Blackwood said concerning this quality in his preaching: "Each sermon he began, not as a traveler asking for the safe route, or inquiring after the opinions held by 'respectable men,' but as a pioneer who thrusts out to find his own way alone." [6] This observation is faulty only in that it implies he went his way "alone," which he did not—for if any preacher ever relied upon the leadership and guidance of the Holy Spirit in his preparation to preach, F. W. Robertson did. Alone humanly speaking, but not alone was he when the Lord's anointing was upon him, as it usually was.

F. W. Robertson combines the qualities of biblical expository method with contemporary, practical, present-day life problems. He seemed to have the rare ability to expound the Scriptures in terms that made them mean something real as they relate to the present, with its present needs. Robertson expressed this goal in a letter to a friend, quoted in Brooke's work, in which he explained that "the great office of the expounder is to adapt old principles to new circumstances and to read the present through the past."

In preaching with the needs of his hearers in view, Robertson chose to preach suggestively rather than dogmatically. His critics came to hear whether or not he repeated the proper words concerning doctrine, but his method was to make religion practical, and he "put doctrine to work" in the lives of those who heard him preach. This of course means that his preaching would best be described as "positive." It was a positive ministry in the sense that he never preached his doubts, but always his convictions. His words were logical, factual, conclusive, and decisive.

He prepared his sermons believing that any passage of scripture must be studied with ourselves in possession of the circumstances under which the words were spoken and with

[5] *Ibid.*, p. 31.
[6] *Op. cit.*, p. 87.

an understanding of how the passage corresponds to our circumstances. He prepared intensively. He was a specific rather than a general reader. His reading was deep rather than wide. In his early ministry he read hundreds of books, which he said "evaporated from" his mind. In his later ministry he read fewer books, read them more slowly and carefully, and made the habit of writing down the abstract of the book's thesis, which he retained in his memory for years.

It was his practice to seek complete seclusion in the preparation of his sermons. His plan, step by step, began with the making of full notes as he proceeded with his research. Then he made an outline as a guide to the development of whatever single purpose he had in mind. His next step was to write his thoughts freely, often making as many as three full manuscripts before he was satisfied he had expressed himself adequately and clearly. His last step was to make a skeleton outline, which he sometimes carried with him into the pulpit. Usually, however, he did not take any notes or manuscript with him into the pulpit when he preached.

His delivery was made effective by the intense feeling behind his words, by his impressive voice, and by a unique phenomenon of "audience rapport" which he seemed to have with his hearers which made them feel that he was talking with each of them individually. Blackwood quoted one of his listeners as saying, "I cannot describe to you in words the strange sensation during his sermon, of union with him and communion with one another which filled us as he spoke." [7]

He seemed to plead with men when he preached. His deep-set blue eyes had an earnest look. One who heard him said of his eyes, "They left their light with you when he had gone." He used few gestures, occasionally lifting a hand or shifting his feet. His posture in the pulpit was flawless. He stood erect, giving the impression of dignity without

[7] *Op. cit.,* p. 118.

cold formality. Blackwood wrote of his delivery that the "most impressive thing about him was his voice, low and musical, full of restrained feeling, in its varied tones and cadences like the voice of the sea."

After a study of five of Robertson's books and three of his biographies, Richard May decided that the secret of his success must be attributed at least to some extent to the intensity with which he preached. There was an indescribable attraction which was beyond his outline, his spoken word, his prepared sermon, his skill of communication. This intensity, it must be concluded, is the result of the anointing and unction of the Holy Spirit.

The intense pace he kept for himself brought about a break in his health in 1852, making him what his friends called "an old man at thirty-six." Each sermon he preached —the majority of them were constructed with two main divisions—took something from his strength. He drove himself relentlessly on, in the many hours of study, the emotionally intense preaching, the conscientious and taxing pastoral care of his flock, and his life burned out on August 16, 1853. The family wanted a private funeral, but the citizens of Brighton claimed Frederick W. Robertson belonged to them also. High and Low Church Anglicans; Roman Catholics, Nonconformists, Jews, Quakers, and Unitarians; rich and poor alike; liberals and conservatives alike—all paid homage to the passing of the beloved pastor of Brighton, whose monument stands as a symbol of faithful pastor, Bible expositor, and brilliant preacher of the word of truth.

CHAPTER 18

Alexander Maclaren

1826-1910

I sometimes think that a verse in one of the psalms carries the whole path of homiletics—"While I was musing the fire burned: then spake I with my tongue." Patient meditation, resulting in kindled emotion and the flashing up of truth into warmth and light, and then—and not until then—the rush of speech "moved by the Holy Ghost." [1]

Thus wrote Alexander Maclaren to his friend Harwood Pattison when the latter requested his opinions on the preparation of sermons which he shared with his students in preaching class—and thus in a few simple words is what might be said to be the philosophy of preaching of one of the great pastors of Scotland's Baptist church of a century ago. Alexander Maclaren made an impact upon those who crowded into his church to hear him preach, and he makes an even greater and more lasting impact upon those who are reading his masterful expositions of the sacred Word today.

Born the youngest in a family of six children to David Maclaren and his godly wife, Mary, in Glasgow in February of 1826, young Alexander received the kind of home training that would fit a man for the ministry. His father, part-time preacher and merchant, and his mother, the daughter of a Scottish Baptist deacon, believed in bringing up their children in the nurture and admonition of the Lord—with liberal quantities of Scottish discipline, strict attention to the teaching of the Bible, and high ideals of Christian ethics. Until his death in Edinburgh in May, 1910, Alexander followed faithfully in the path of piety to which his good parents had inspired him.

Sent by the authorities of Stepney College to supply the pulpit for one Sunday at Portland Chapel in Southampton,

---

[1] E. T. Maclaren, *Alexander Maclaren of Manchester* (New York: The Macmillan Company, 1911).

Alexander Maclaren (he signed his name McLaren, but used the more formal spelling in all his published works) was invited to accept the church as his permanent charge. At the age of nineteen he became the pastor of a church which, although at the time was on the downward trend, presented a challenging opportunity to one so young. Typical of his keen Scottish sense of humor was Maclaren's remark soon after beginning his pastorate here: "If the worst comes to the worst I shall at all events not have to reflect that I have killed a flourishing plant but only assisted at the funeral of a withered one." [2]

There was no "funeral" of this withered plant of a church. Gradually but steadily his congregation grew in number and influence until at the end of eight years at Southampton he filled the chapel both morning and evening on Sunday, and there were some two hundred persons in the midweek services. This was the result, largely, of his preaching. The people of his charge did not seem to feel much need for extensive pastoral visitation, and Alexander Maclaren used relatively little of his precious time in visiting with his flock. He spent many hours in careful preparation for his preaching ministry.

After eleven years as a bachelor pastor in Southampton, Alexander Maclaren was married to a distant cousin, Marion, and the two lived a happy life with the two daughters whom God gave them to increase the loveliness of their home.

When the call came to serve the larger church at Manchester, Maclaren accepted, after some thirteen years at Southampton, although he did so reluctantly, feeling that there was much more to be done in his first charge. His biographer, E. T. Maclaren, suggested that it was here in Manchester that his preaching developed into the form of biblical exposition which characterized it throughout his ministry. The people of this church were hungry for Bible teaching, and their able pastor saw to it that they received it in his Sunday messages. It was while serving this church

[2] *Ibid.*

that Alexander Maclaren decried what he called "the rubbish of intellectual preaching," and it was here that he made Christ live in his sermons.

Maclaren's biblical emphasis is seen in his excellent expository sermons, which he seemed never to tire of preparing and which his listeners seemed never to grow weary of hearing. This quality is seen also in the illustrative material which found its way into his messages. He rarely used outside illustrative ideas—he used illustrations from the Scripture itself, or made such applications of his points that no illustrations were necessary. For example, in his sermon, "A Sheaf of Prayer Arrows," from the text Ps. 86: 1-5, he uses no other source than the Bible for his illustrations. In "The Lesson of Memory," the title he gives his sermon on Deut. 8:2, he uses three illustrations in the subdivisions of his first point. They are taken from the life of Moses, the folly of the Egyptians, and the life of Jacob. There is no illustrative material in this sermon outside biblical sources.

It may be observed also that many of his introductions are contextual in nature, adding this much more to the mighty mass of scriptural content of his preaching.

Alexander Maclaren was one of the first to exploit the idea of the "parallel sermon." In his first pastorate he often preached on a given subject in the morning and its parallel or counterpart in the evening. For example, in one of his morning services he preached on "The Necessity of Companionship," and that evening his sermon was "The Advantages of Solitude."

One observes another evidence of Maclaren's originality in his departure from the accepted customs of his day when he deemed it advisable. The people of Manchester were accustomed to the traditional "carrying up of the Bible and hymnbook" to indicate that the service was about to begin. Maclaren would have none of this; he, at the punctual moment, simply opened the vestry door and slowly mounted the steps to the pulpit. He departed from the custom in his manner of remaining in his seat to sing with the congregation rather than mounting the pulpit to do so. He desired, as he put it, "To join in the praise, not lead it."

His public prayer and reading of the Bible were as carefully prepared and faultlessly performed as his preaching, although he cast aside his previously prepared thoughts when he prayed, so that he might "remember nothing but that I am speaking to God for others and for myself and that He is listening." Those who heard him declared that from the tone of his voice he never did forget that God was listening.

His reading of the Word was done with such feeling and interpretation that some people actually came to church just to hear him read the Scriptures. The Bible was to him a book of such eternal truth and wonder that the attention of his hearers was drawn like a magnet to steel when he read it.

The author of the book *Dr. Maclaren of Manchester* suggested that it is difficult to describe the preaching of this great pastor.

We may speak of the spare figure quivering with life and feeling; of the firm set mouth, the unmistakable sign of a tremendous will; of eyes that pierce and shine and seem to compass everybody and everything in their quick, lightning glance; or of the strangely magnetic voice—but in vain. We may describe his preaching as "logic on fire," or say that his words thrill like electricity; that he speaks like one wholly possessed by his theme, or that that speaker's *tout ensemble* gives one of the best idea possible of etheralized matter, of spirit overpowering matter; but it fails.[3]

Maclaren never wrote out his sermons to be delivered from manuscript. He preached from notes, extemporaneously. He aimed to maintain contact with his audience and was surprisingly successful in achieving what some have called rapport with his listeners. To have read his sermons would have meant, in his opinion, sacrificing this valuable condition for preaching. His use of a brief outline and reliance on his extensive experience with books and the

[3] Maclaren, *op. cit.*

reality of life, coupled with the dynamic power of the Holy Spirit, resulted in what he called "pushing out from the shore and launching into deep water." It was an effective method of delivery for Alexander Maclaren.

His outlines were usually easy to see, and not hard to follow. For example, his sermon from Mark 2:19, "And Jesus said unto them, Can the children of the bridechamber fast, while the bridegroom is with them?" is given under the title "The Secret of Gladness." His main divisions, which are punctuated with smooth and clearly indicated transitional sentences, are:

    I. The Bridegroom
   II. The Presence of the Bridegroom
  III. The Joy of the Bridegroom's Presence[4]

His style was often vivid, always clear, never dull. He would speak of "a length of the fox's skin of deceit," or of "an airy phantom in the brain of a single sobbing woman." His listeners were captivated by the language he used. But more important, he spoke like one anointed and blessed by the Holy Spirit. All this made his preaching great.

"While I was musing the fire burned: then I spake with my tongue." It is a good thing for those who heard him that the fire burned in the soul of this saintly Scot. It burned, and he spoke with his tongue. It was an eloquent tongue, but more, the burning and speaking were in the spirit of a man wholly possessed by his theme. What more is there to be said of the preaching of any man?

[4] Alexander Maclaren, *Expositions of the Holy Scriptures, St. Mark* (Grand Rapids, Mich.: William B. Eerdmans Company, 1944), VIII, 75-86.

CHAPTER 19

Charles Haddon Spurgeon

1834-92

"You may write my life across the
skies. I have nothing to conceal."
So spoke a tired but happy fifty-eight-year-old preacher
shortly before his death. And so wrote a host of biographers,
students, preachers, and scholars who have "written his
life across the skies" and have indeed found nothing that
should be concealed. Conwell, Cook, Day, Ellis, Fuller,
Lorimer, Needham, Pike, Shindler—how many more have
found it worthwhile to record the life and ministry of
Charles Haddon Spurgeon? How many have been inspired
and blessed as they have learned of his devotion to Christ,
his passion for the lost, his love of humanity, his pulpit
eloquence, his skill of biblical exposition?

Born at Kelvedon, in Essex, England, in 1834, Spurgeon
was the son and grandson of preachers. His father was a
businessman, but preached for sixteen years to a small
congregation of independents. His grandfather, James
Spurgeon, served as the pastor at Stambourne, in Essex,
for more than fifty years.

Always religious-minded, Charles nevertheless felt deep
conviction for about a year before his conversion, which
took place in a definite crisis experience when he was
fifteen. It was not long afterward that he preached his first
sermon at the age of sixteen, and at seventeen he was pastor
of his first charge. Richard Day writes of his first year at
Waterbeach, "He accepted the call after many hours of
prayer. The salary was fixed at $225 a year; insufficient to
keep him, but the good people brought him bread, produce,
and always thought of him when they killed a pig."

After serving at Waterbeach for something less than
three years, he received and accepted a call to the New Park
Street Church in London. Here he served as pastor for over
thirty years, and here he published a weekly sermon con-

tinuously from 1855 until his death in 1892, without losing his freshness and originality.

This story went the rounds of shop, classroom, and parlor during Spurgeon's ministry: It seems a certain young lad was being quizzed by a stranger, who asked the boy who the prime minister of England was. "Mr. Spurgeon!" the boy replied emphatically. And perhaps the boy was correct, for Charles Haddon Spurgeon was indeed the "prime" minister of his country during those eventful years.

Opposed vigorously during those first months of his ministry to the largest nonconformist church in Britain, Spurgeon won his critics slowly but surely to an appreciation for his right to lead the congregation. One finds it difficult to analyze the opposition, which was at times bordering upon the extravagant and the emotional. Perhaps it was his boyish appearance, which brought people to hear him because of the novelty of it. Perhaps it was what people mistakenly thought was immaturity, for he married after he had been serving as pastor in London for only about two years. But Russell E. Conwell in his biography of Spurgeon observed that his persecution helped him rather than hindered, for many came to scoff, yet they recognized in the young preacher a confidence "born of confidence in God" as he spoke as one having authority.

An anonymous writer described Spurgeon as being

somewhat below the middle height, with heavy features and a curious inequality in his eyes . . . the heavy eyes beamed with benevolence . . . there was a gleam of fun in almost every glance, and the impression his looks created was not only that of an honest and kindly nature, but of a genial and witty intelligence.

His hair, thick and black, was worn long and parted in the middle. The voluminous collar and tie that swathed his short neck did not lend dignity to the wearer. In later life his looks improved with the mellowness of experience, and it was said "he was always pleasant to look upon, and was always neat and well-groomed in appearance."

An individualist, Spurgeon was never one to be led around

by the nose in his relation with his deacons. Soon after his coming to London his congregation had swelled in size until Spurgeon mentioned in the pulpit that soon the walls would have to be knocked out and the building enlarged. After the sermon one of the deacons approached the young preacher and told him they "would hear no more of it." Spurgeon abruptly replied that they would hear no more of it when it was done!

Andrew W. Blackwood has suggested that Spurgeon's use of the Scriptures played a significant part in his effectiveness as a preacher. He quoted Spurgeon as saying that it is often the text, not the sermon, that saves the sinner. In examining the sermons of C. H. Spurgeon, one believes he practiced this philosophy. Most of his introductions are based on the text and context. Many of his illustrations are from the Bible. His divisions are, for the most part, a development of textual, inferential, or expository nature. His knowledge of the Scriptures is quickly apparent, and with this unusual knowledge is seen also a consuming love for the Bible. This transfers itself to the reader of Spurgeon's sermons, as it most certainly must have done to those who heard him.

A significant characteristic of Spurgeon's preaching, in addition to its biblical content, is the evangelistic fervor with which he delivered his sermons. Lorimer stated that "he always planned for immediate results. He expected someone to be renovated or bettered by the words that fell from his lips."

Blackwood also saw this factor in Spurgeon's preaching, pointing out that in a volume of twelve sermons by Spurgeon, which were intended to be pastoral, they would "in present day terms be evangelistic." After each of the twelve is a printed appeal "to the unconverted hearer."

There was an intense moral earnestness in the preaching of Spurgeon which is particularly noteworthy and which doubtless accounted, at least in part, for a measure of his evangelistic success. He was possessed with a passion for souls. His voice often broke into sobs, and tears streamed from his eyes as he pleaded with the unconverted to be reconciled to God. One of his listeners declares that he sometimes preached in such agony that he could not keep his foot on the floor, but had to sit on a chair and prop his foot on another chair while speaking. No wonder such fervor had an effect on those who heard him.

Yet another factor in the effectiveness of his preaching was his spirit of prayer. Lorimer put it aptly when he stated, "He preached well because he prayed well." James J. Ellis said of his prayers that they "have been a means of grace and a revelation of what prayer might more often be . . . prayers which ring in his heart still, and mingle with his holiest purposes, which indeed that inspired." [1] His prayers in public services are said to have had a simplicity and directness, together with a subdued fervor and a child-like confidence, which made it seem that he was "talking with God reverently and humbly as became a creature, yet boldly and trustfully as became a saint." It has been said that Spurgeon attributed the success of his ministry to the fact that people were praying while he preached.

Homiletically, Spurgeon seemed to practice a system of reasoning from the known to the unknown, as Conwell has pointed out. The divisions of his sermons are clear and distinct. He announced them, and he emphasized them. It was easy to reproduce them in substance for some days after listening to them. The divisions served as a set of "pegs" upon which to hang the truths and illustrations which came under them.

An example of the divisions of his sermons is seen in "Songs in the Night," preached from the text in Job 35:10 "But none saith, Where is God my maker, who giveth songs in the night?" It is:

I. Songs in the night—their source. God giveth them.
II. Songs in the night—their matter. What do we sing about in the night?
III. Songs in the night—their excellence. They are hearty songs and sweet songs.

[1] *Charles Haddon Spurgeon* (London: J. Nisbet & Company, 1891).

IV. Songs in the night—their uses. Their benefits to ourselves and others.[2]

Spurgeon used many illustrations. He quoted Baxter, Shakespeare, Dante, and Bunyan. He gave personal illustrations. He quoted poetry. In the sermon "The Leafless Tree" there are eight quotations of poetry; in "Songs in the Night" there are seven.

Vivid style kept the truth fresh and powerful. He declared: "The orchestra shall be composed of damned men, and howling fiends, and yelling demons." In another sermon he said, "Fair professors once they were; they stood green among the church, like the very leaves of paradise; but in an evil hour they fell, the slaves of temptation."

Robert Wilmot studied the preaching of C. H. Spurgeon and noted his conversational manner at the outset, his soft, melodious pleadings and strong denunciations, with all the various tones, some of which cut like a knife and others as fragrant and tender as a mother's kiss. But he decided the secret of his power lay in his saturation with the Scriptures.

To this all must agree, but to this may well be added one more thing—his Christ-centered message. Some of the first words of Spurgeon in the Metropolitan Tabernacle, after the congregation had moved into their new sanctuary in March, 1861, show this vital element in his preaching:

I would propose that the subject of the ministry of this house, as long as this platform shall stand, shall be the person of Jesus Christ . . . if I am asked what is my creed, I must reply, "It is Jesus Christ" . . . Christ Jesus who is the sum and substance of the gospel, the incarnation of every previous truth, the all glorious embodiment of the way, the truth, and the life.[3]

[2] Blackwood, *The Protestant Pulpit*, pp. 114-28.
[3] Richard Ellsworth Day, *The Shadow of the Broad Brim* (Philadelphia: Judson Press, 1934), p. 218.

CHAPTER 20

Phillips Brooks
1835-93

I had rather hear you praised for
holiness than for talent, though of
course that is unspeakably precious when used in good service.
But, my dear Philly, let no human praise make you proud, but
be humble as the Master you serve, and never forget what an
honor it is to be the servant of Christ.[1]

So wrote a godly and devoted woman to her preacher son,
a son whose strikingly attractive physique and uniquely
appealing manner were winning for him popular acclaim
such as few ministers had received in his generation. That
son was Phillips Brooks.

It would not be accurate to attribute his popularity as
a preacher to physique or manner, however. As a matter of
fact, there would necessarily be many factors which could
explain the effectiveness of his preaching, and perhaps most
of them were of greater importance than these. The inclination to magnify these traits of personality comes as a result
of his own definition of preaching, which has been quoted
by many authors of books on homiletics since he stated it
in his lectures to Yale divinity students: "These are the
elements of preaching—Truth and Personality." He insisted
there must always be a proper balance between the two
elements and advised, "Let a man be a true preacher,
really uttering the truth through his own personality, and
it is strange how men will gather to listen to him." [2]

Born in Boston on December 13, 1835, he attended Adams
school and Boston Latin school and was graduated from
Harvard College at the age of twenty. After having taught
for a year in Boston Latin school, he attended Alexandria

[1] William Lawrence, *Life of Phillips Brooks* (New York: Harper
& Brothers, 1930), p. 68.
[2] Phillips Brooks, *Lectures On Preaching* (Grand Rapids, Mich.
Zondeman Publishing House, n.d.), pp. 5 ff.

Theological Seminary, where he was graduated in 1859. It was a year later that he was ordained in the Episcopal ministry, and he began preaching at the age of twenty-three. His first ten years of pastoral ministry were spent in Philadelphia. He spent a year abroad, and became rector of Trinity Church in Boston in 1869. It was here that he became prominently known, and it was here that he accomplished his most fruitful ministry. With the exception of his trips abroad and his occasional lectureships in Harvard, he served this parish until his election as Bishop of Massachusetts two years before his death in 1893. Thirty-four of his fifty-eight years were spent preaching, and his preaching remains an example which twentieth century pastors and evangelists may well strive to follow.

Phillips Brooks possessed strong character. A. W. Thorold, the English Bishop of Winchester, described him as "strong, fearless, tender, eloquent, incapable of meanness, blazing with indignation at all kinds of wrong." Reserved yet cheerful, he impressed all who knew him with his quiet strength of spirit. One who traveled with him abroad said later that he was perennially cheerful. He was not often alone, yet he seemed hungry for human affection.

He never married. He said of himself that although his life was one of the happiest, he considered the mistake of his life was not to have married. He missed the companionship of a wife and the experience of enjoying a family.

Brooks was deeply conscientious, not only in his dealings with others, but also in his attitude toward himself. He observed great neatness in his dress, but avoided every badge of his calling in the way he dressed. He would not allow himself to be photographed in his clerical garb because he considered it too sacred. He was conscientious in the way he answered his correspondence, answering letters so promptly his friends hesitated to write him for fear of adding to his burden. He was conscientious in entering every door of opportunity that opened to him. He once declared that he had never declined any invitation to preach unless he was prevented by a previous invitation or by illness. He had the soul of a poet and often wrote the poetry he read in his sermons. A reading of his published manuscripts reveals frequent quotations of poetry. Not many people associate him with the famous Christmas carol "O Little Town of Bethlehem," which he wrote in 1868 largely because of his love for children. His organist, Lewis Redner, urged him to write a carol, and he agreed with the provision that Redner should write the music.

Unusual in his day was the work he did in parish calling. He spent much of every afternoon in calling and once stated at a meeting of clergy where preaching was extolled and pastoral calling deprecated, "I would like to do nothing but make pastoral calls and meet the people. Indeed, if I did not, I could not preach!" [3] It was doubtless his personality and experience with life which affected his preaching at least equally as much as his brilliant intellect and thorough preparation.

Phillips Brooks's preaching was a departure from the usual in his time. He congregations were often amazed at the preaching which was so unlike any that they had heard before. The old familiar gospel story was there, but his delivery was different and his words were stripped of the old clichés, the usual conventionalities, and the threadbare expressions. There was a unique combination of scholarly dignity with folksy simplicity. His preaching was at the same time profound and simple—profound in thought, but simple in language. Biographer DeWolfe Howe claims that the same sermon Brooks might preach at Wellesley College he could also preach at Concord State Prison. His secret seems to have been in his methods of using timeless, eternal truths in his messages, yet illustrating and applying them in the light of events in the lives of his listeners. He knew their needs and he understood their problems; this made his preaching meaningful for those who heard him.

Brooks's thorough preaching preparation was made pos-

[3] Lawrence, *op. cit.*, p. 48.

sible by his gift of rapid reading. He could take in a page of printed material in a very small amount of time. His home was filled with books—and where there were no books there were pictures. The ability to read rapidly, coupled with an active imagination and keen memory, enriched and freshened his ministry. Without plagiarism, he was able to use what he learned. It is said that someone asked Charles Lamb where he got the material for one of his essays and he replied, "I milked three hundred cows for it; but the butter is mine!" So might have said Phillips Brooks. He read widely as well as wisely, and he "churned his own butter."

Brooks wrote every sermon out in full each week, and sometimes wrote also his Wednesday night lectures and his other addresses. He did not always read from the manuscript as his method of delivery. He had the ability to retain so much of what he had read and pondered that it was not necessary that he be bound to his manuscript. He spoke extremely rapidly. Biographer William Lawrence says he plunged immediately into his delivery at full speed, and it was not easy for the audience to keep up with him. While the average preacher speaks at the rate of some 120 words per minute, Phillips Brooks spoke at the rate of from 190 to 215 words per minute!

He would announce his text in a rather quiet voice, sometimes too low to reach all corners of a large sanctuary. A gradual increase in volume accompanied the delivery of his sermons. The speed of his delivery, however, remained almost as rapid from the beginning to the close. A very remarkable clearness in enunciation, fortunately, diminished the difficulty of keeping pace with his extraordinary speed.

One writer, in a study of Brooks, points out that in his later ministry there was a depth of emotion that was not present in the beginning. There were many times that he showed visible signs of his own deep feelings while his words moved the emotions of his audience. The people who heard him seemed more deeply moved than they were in his earlier years and seemed to want *him*, rather than his eloquence or his gifts.

His sermons were largely topical in development, but some of them were textual. His introductions were always brief and usually contextual in their content. Sometimes he used the background leading up to the text and sometimes found his introduction in the text itself. Most often, his outline was the development of the topic he found there, but not necessarily the material to be found within the text. The text itself was his springboard from which he leaped out into the treatment of the truth which was his message.

His conclusions were usually an application of the truth of his message. One feels moved even today after reading his sermons, although it is true that a written sermon seldom reveals half the actual spirit one feels when he hears it preached.

One of his best-known sermons is entitled "The Fire and the Calf" in which he used the text in Exod. 32:24: "So they gave it to me: then I cast it into the fire, and there came out this calf." He showed, in his first point, what this statement of Aaron represents—it was a deliberate lie told by a man who was afraid to face the truth. His next point showed what this means—Aaron was really deceiving himself more than anyone else; men today often blame their hands and not their hearts for the sins they have committed. His final point described the cure—until a man takes the responsibility for his sins he will be unable to find forgiveness. In his conclusion he appealed to his listeners to confess they had sinned and to seek God's forgiveness!

Today there stands a statue of Phillips Brooks before Trinity Church in Boston. One can see in the likeness of this saintly minister something of the dignity of his tall, six-feet-four-inch frame and his compassionate character. Behind the statue of the preacher there is another figure— the Christ he preached hovers behind and above him with his hand on Brooks's shoulder. It is the Christ he exalted who made his preaching great, and it is that same Christ who wants to bless the ministry of all, as we, like Phillips Brooks, give him the best of our service.

CHAPTER 21

Dwight L. Moody
1837-99

> Spurgeon was called the pastoral evangelist; Chalmers, the parish evangelist; Finney, the revival evangelist; Howard, the prison evangelist; Whitefield, the field evangelist; Shaftesbury, the philanthropic evangelist; Bliss, the singing evangelist; McCauley, the evangelist of the outcast; but Dwight L. Moody was the evangelist of the people.[1]

So wrote J. W. Hanson in his *Life and Works of Dwight L. Moody,* and so agrees the student who thoughtfully reads Moody's sermons and carefully examines his preaching.

Dwight L. Moody was not a great preacher as some preachers would count greatness, for he violated many of their ideas about homiletics; but he was a great preacher when the results are brought into focus and the principles of preaching recede into a less conspicuous view, for he preached in a way that captivated the interest of his listeners and in a way that brought men to Christ. Even the most particular student of preaching must admit this is enough to account Moody worthy of distinction as a great preacher of the gospel.

Born in Northfield, Massachusetts, in 1837, Dwight L. Moody was one of a family of nine children in a home that had for two centuries seen its family produce preachers of note. There was Joshua Moody in the seventeenth century and Samuel Moody in the eighteenth century, and of course Dwight L. Moody's preaching is one of the bright spots in a nineteenth century preoccupied with wealth and growth.

The early childhood of Dwight Moody and his family was characterized by hardship and disappointment. His father died when Dwight was four, and the boy fought hard to help his mother provide for the family. At sixteen, he was making a name for himself as a shoe salesman. He overcame

[1] Chicago: W. B. Conkey, 1900, p. 5.

personal obstacles, such as the awkwardness of long, lean, lanky adolescence and a tendency to stammer when nervous, and developed skill in meeting people through salesmanship. This experience doubtless influenced his ministry as "the people's evangelist."

Moody's conversion is well known to every Christian. One cannot forget the thrill of knowing how that obscure Sunday-school teacher, Edward Kimball, spoke to Dwight in the back of a Boston shoe store in such compelling, convicting force that the two were soon on their knees in prayer. Moody tearfully gave his heart to Jesus, and Kimball wept and murmured his thanks to God! D. L. Moody at eighteen found an experience that changed the course of his life.

Harry J. Albus, writing about Moody in *A Treasury of Dwight L. Moody*, tells of his moving to Chicago a year after his conversion in search of a fortune in salesmanship. Had he devoted his energies primarily toward achieving that goal rather than toward the winning of souls, he most certainly would have become a wealthy man. He possessed the ability to make money. His foresight, his enthusiasm, his perseverance, his intelligence and cleverness, and his effectiveness in sales work would have been in his favor. He put God first, however, and God had work for him to do. He organized a Sunday-school class of eighteen youngsters, which grew eventually into a class of over a thousand. He severed all business ties to give his full time to soul winning.

Moody was a personal evangelist as well as an evangelistic preacher. Long before the demands came for his great public meetings, he was busy distributing Bibles, books, and tracts, organizing "Bands of Brothers" among his converts, and training them to carry the gospel to others. He organized noon prayer meetings, visited workers in their jobs and soldiers in their barracks, and spoke to strangers on the street corners. Every day he was busy winning men to Christ.

Perhaps this explains why Moody became a great mass evangelist, for when he preached to thousands he preached as though he were talking with one individual. That individual felt the impact of the message, and he—and hundreds of others like him—moved to seek salvation.

Moody's preaching was clear. The most intelligent person in the audience gave rapt attention, but the humblest and least educated and the smallest child also heard and understood. The children were among the most eager of his listeners. Few men have been able to attain the art of convincing the old and at the same time captivating the young, as did Moody.

D. L. Moody believed what he preached. His faith was the faith of a little child, and he believed absolutely and implicitly in the message he preached. There was no laziness in his body or spirit.

Oratory was natural with him, but he did not seek to use it consciously. He knew how to make an illustration live vividly, and he was more than ordinarily emotional, especially in his climax, but it was not affected nor artificial. He loved anecdotes, Bible stories, analogies, or anything that helped make his points clear. His descriptive powers were far above average, and he used imagination in the best sense.

Moody knew how to make use of his keen sense of humor without cheapening the content of his preaching. He used pathos mixed with humor. From laughing to weeping, his audiences moved with him in the sort of attentive rapport every preacher covets and few realize.

D. L. Moody's introductions were perhaps the best examples of his violations of the rules of homiletics—but he did well anyway. W. E. Sangster declared that it is impossible to exaggerate the importance of the beginning of a sermon, and Charles E. Jefferson once wrote that if a man cannot say anything in the first ten minutes of his sermon he ought to drop the first ten and begin with the second ten! Moody sometimes had little or no introduction at all, and at other times made two or three false starts—unforgivable in homiletics class—but his lovable and attractive personality plus his perfect submission to the Holy Spirit made up for it.

Moody was primarily a topical preacher. In his sermon, often preached at the beginning of a revival, "Stones to Be Rolled Away," he began with a rather lengthy introduction and then gave some of the stones that needed to be rolled away if God would give a revival. The stone of unbelief, the stone of prejudice, and the stone of sectarian spirit marked the three main divisions.

Probably his best-known and greatest sermon was "What Think Ye of Christ?" from the text in Matt. 22:42. The introduction was, as might be expected, much too long according to all the rules, but one must admit it is interesting and captivating. Such an expression as "But these are not the points I wish to take up" characterized his beginnings in the sermon. His main divisions were:

I. What think ye of Christ as a Teacher?
II. What think ye of Christ as a Physician?
III. What think ye of Christ as a Comforter? [2]

He used gestures moderately, but his language was the language that gripped the hearts and minds of the people. "I would rather be narrow and right, than broad and wrong," he would say—with eleven words, nine of which were of one syllable, he drove the point forcefully across. He would say, "Ahab had influence; Elijah had power"; "If you want results, just pray."

As a matter of fact, Moody was right and not narrow. The Moody stereotype, promoted by some of his followers, is that of a narrow literalist. On the contrary, his fostering of education in the establishment of Northfield and Mt. Hermon, his high popularity in the American and British universities, and his strong friendship with great liberals such as George Adam Smith and Henry Drummond show that he was right and not narrow.

After one writer made a study of Moody's ministry, he attempted to summarize his personal characteristics:

[2] Blackwood, *The Protestant Pulpit,* pp. 138-43.

He must have believed all he preached. . . . He was humble, consistent in Christian experience, able to firmly stand alone, modest, simple in mode and manner, courageous, strong, stable, impulsive, direct, analytical, peaceful, determined, intense in convictions, able to rebuke, quick in perception, a hero worshipper, and a diligent, consecrated servant of Jesus Christ.[3]

The keynote of his ministry was struck in the experience he had of hearing the statement made, "It remains to be seen what God can do if He can find a man who will completely surrender to Him!" Dwight L. Moody thought about that statement awhile and fervently murmured, "I will be that man."

He preached in every large city in America, in four campaigns in England, in missions and slums on Skid Row, in well-appointed churches and well-filled auditoriums, and in that very last revival campaign in Kansas City, which he was unable to finish—his last before his death. The results of this preaching would all indicate that his fervent prayer was answered. Dwight L. Moody "was that man."

[3] William R. Moody, *The Life of Dwight L. Moody* (New York: Fleming H. Revell Company, 1900), pp. 512 ff.

CHAPTER 22

Frederick B. Meyer

1847-1929

"I am only an ordinary man. I
have no special gifts. I am no
orator, no scholar, no profound thinker. If I have done anything for Christ and my generation, it is because I have
given myself entirely to Christ Jesus, and then tried to do
whatever He wanted me to do." [1]

Thus spoke a man whose preaching has inspired ministers
of the gospel to be expositors rather than entertainers, Bible-
centered preachers rather than topic-centered teachers,
dedicated students of the Word rather than casual tasters
of truth. These are the words of a man whose life and
ministry embodied the ideals of Christ-centered, Bible-
saturated, spirit-anointed pastoral preaching—Frederick
Brotherton Meyer.

Born in London on April 8, 1847, F. B. Meyer was blessed
with godly parents and a happy home. His religious heritage
was enriched with the influence of his Quaker grandmother,
whose holy life made a lasting impression upon him during
his most formative years. Meyer is quoted by Chester Mann
as having declared concerning his early home life, "I believe
that a man can bear any losses, any sorrow or disappointment, if he has in the background of his mind the beautiful
picture of a Christian home. My whole life is embosomed in
lovely associations connected with my childhood at Chap-
ham." [2]

Frederick Meyer believed in his earliest childhood that
he would someday preach the Word. He accepted as matter
of fact the remark his pastor made on Sunday morning
while greeting the congregation at the close of the morning
service. As he shook the hand of his youthful member he

[1] A. Chester Mann, *F. B. Meyer* (New York: Fleming H. Revell
Company, 1929), p. 23.
[2] *Ibid.*, p. 33.

said, "Someday you will stand at the end of the aisle and shake hands with the people, as I am doing now." This bit of prophecy was fulfilled sooner than either of them thought possible; Meyer was called to preach at the age of sixteen.

Even earlier than his call, however, he seemed always to believe that he would someday preach. He often "played at preaching" with his small brothers and sisters as the audience. On one occasion a housemaid heard one of the lad's "sermons" and was convicted of her need of Christ, and she dates her conversion as a result of that experience.

The preparation of F. B. Meyer for his lifework included two years in a tea merchant's office, which taught him valuable lessons about the world of trade and commerce, and his studies at Regent's Park College and London University. The latter conferred upon him the bachelor of arts degree in 1869, soon after his twenty-second birthday.

Meyer's pastoral ministry was both versatile and fruitful. He served for a year as a student pastor in Richmond, and upon graduation he accepted an assistant pastorate under the able Dr. C. M. Birrell at Pembroke Chapel in Liverpool. It was while he lived here that he met and married Miss Jane Eliza Jones.

The outstanding term of his pastoral ministry was spent in Christ Church, Lambeth, where he served fifteen years, from 1892 until 1907; then from 1915 until 1920, another term of five years. When he began his work there, the average Sundy evening attendance was about one hundred, but within a few years the sanctuary was often filled to its capacity of more than two thousand. In his first four years as pastor there the membership doubled in number.

It is most interesting to observe the influences that helped to mold the methods of this man who became one of England's great pastoral preachers. There was in his early ministry, under the influence of the strong, dynamic personality of Dr. Birrell, a tendency which he later admitted and decried but which persisted until he left Liverpool. It was a tendency to imitate Dr. Birrell. J. H. Shakespeare, in writing his observations in one of Meyer's biographies, said:

"Birrell's personality was altogether too strong, and it was not until Meyer had shaken off a kind of idolatrous imitation of his senior that the young minister manifested something of his own power." [3]

Another significant change in his development as a preacher occurred in his method of preparation. In his early ministry he patterned his methods ofter that of Dr. Birrell and of John Henry Jowett, writing every sermon in full, with careful meticulous attention to polish and balance of style, then committing the manuscript to memory for delivery. He declared later that he destroyed countless reams of paper in writing, correcting, and revising his sermons during those early years. He often spent three or four hours writing the introduction alone!

This method of preparation was not his own and admittedly was not a natural one to his style of preaching. Chester Mann quoted Meyer as saying, "This method was totally unsuitable to me." In his later ministry he used a method more natural to his own needs. He did not forsake the habit or writing sermons in their entirety, but he did change his method of memorizing and delivering the sermons he preached. His new method began with the selection of his text early in the week, so as to allow time for its consideration. He would write down thoughts on note paper, and read whatever helpful materials were available. The main message of the sermon soon became apparent. He described the process:

One feels that this is the burden of the Lord for the coming service. . . . I have known cases where the outline did not appear clearly until within an hour or two of preaching, but when that is the case, it does not greatly concern me. One comes to trust a series of automatic processes by which the mind will ultimately evolve the message and its ordering.[4]

It was when Meyer began to preach extemporaneously

[3] *Ibid.*, p. 42.
[4] F. B. Meyer, *Hints For Lay Preachers* (New York: Fleming H. Revell Company, 1928), p. 76.

that his delivery became most effective, according to those who heard him. His early method of writing his sermons resulted in accuracy of style and in sharp beauty of expression, but his delivery was the key to his power in the pulpit.

Cicero declared concerning this vital phase of speaking: "Without effective delivery a speaker of the highest mental capacity can be held in no esteem, while one of moderate abilities, with this qualification, may surpass even those of the highest talent." Meyer's delivery must have satisfied those who would agree with Cicero, for Principal Thomas Phillips wrote of his preaching:

I have heard Dr. Meyer preach many times. Sometimes his stuff was great, but whether great or ordinary, he always "got it across." He wove a spell over his audience. Not so learned as Dr. Clifford, not so concentrated as Hugh Price Hughes, he was undoubtedly one of the greatest preachers of the generation.[5]

Hugh Sinclair in his book *Voices of Today* described F. B. Meyer as looking "exceedingly youthful as he stands, slim and straight, with the glow of the supreme vision upon his face. An engaging intimacy and pastoral touch give a welcome homeliness to his utterance; a gift of evoking the spiritual atmosphere makes awe and magic about him." [6]

It was early in his ministry, under the influence of Dr. Birrell, that F. B. Meyer caught the challenge of expository preaching. Birrell once told his young assistant, "If you make topical sermons your model, you will presently come to the end of your topics, and where will you be then? I advise you to do as I have done for the last thirty years, become an expositor of the Scripture." [7] This he did, and later advised others to do. In his own work *Expository Preaching* Meyer stated: "Expository preaching should have a very conspicuous place. It should be the standing dish; nay, it is the table on which all the dishes are placed." [8]

In analyzing Meyer's expository preaching, one is re-

[5] Mann, *op. cit.*, p. 78.
[6] London: James Clark & Company, 1912.
[7] Mann, *op. cit.*, p. 74.
[8] Garden City, N. Y.: George H. Doran Company, 1912.

minded of Harry E. Jessop's comparison of the various types of sermons. He explained: "In topical preaching you use a rake, gathering from everywhere; in textual preaching you use a knife, cutting and dissecting the parts here and there; in expository preaching you use a spade, digging deeper and deeper into the meaning of the Word." [9] Frederick B. Meyer indeed used a "spade," and the nuggets of rich ore he unearthed have inspired many others to use this method.

No man's preaching power can be explained or understood, however, apart from his own spirit and his own character. Carl W. Baker captured this thought when he observed concerning F. B. Meyer's preaching, "His great power emerges out of the depths of a life hidden in God." Meyer's life behind his words gave them power as he laid them upon the altar, and the Holy Spirit blessed and anointed the sacrifice. In contrast to the man Charles Spurgeon once described as preaching so well and living so badly that when he was in the pulpit everybody said he ought never to come out again, and when he was out of it they decided he ought never to enter it again, Meyer practiced what he preached.

Just six weeks before his death at the age of eighty-two, he preached his last sermon. There were seventy-seven years between his first prayer and his last sermon, sixty-six years from the beginning of his ministry until its end. He lived a great life—great in the light of his own earlier declaration of what he considered makes a great life. He had expressed his thoughts in that respect:

> To fulfill faithfully the duties of your ministry; to bear chaffing and travail as martyrs bore the pillory and stake . . . to love with the love of God even the unthankful and evil; to content to be a fountain in the midst of a wild valley of stones, nourish a few lichens and wild flowers, or now and again a thirsty sheep; and to do this always, and not for the praise of man, but for the sake of God—this makes a great life.[10]

[9] Unpublished Lecture, Nazarene Theological Seminary.
[10] F. B. Meyer, "What Makes A Great Life," reprint in *Preacher's Magazine,* vol. 20, No. 6 (November-December 1945), p. 28.

CHAPTER 23

G. Campbell Morgan
1863-1945

"A Bible expositor without peer. In his hands the Bible—its pages, precepts, characters—is made positively to live and to exude an enheartening, a vital force." [1]

The "expositor without peer" of whom John Harries wrote was a preacher named George Campbell Morgan, whose name has become an inspiration and a challenge to every preacher of the Word who recognizes excellence and appreciates greatness in the most important task of a minister of the gospel of Christ—his preaching.

Born into the home of a humble, itinerant preacher in Cutwell Villa, Tatbury, in Gloucester County, England, in December of 1863, George Campbell Morgan was too frail as a young child to go to school. He received excellent tutoring at home, and although deprived of the social life the public schools would have afforded him, he learned perhaps more during these early years than would have been possible in the schools.

At eight years of age he experienced the first great sorrow of his life when his favorite sister died, but after a normal period of grief he began to find solace in the friendship of other children. About this time his health permitted him to attend the public schools.

Biographer Jill Morgan wrote that his childhood was lived in the "atmosphere of preaching." "Plain living," she explained, "and an absence of all counterattractions, few friends of his own age, together with a sensitive nature which had already felt the basic shock of loss, combined to make him thoughtful and introspective beyond his years."

He preached his first sermon at the age of thirteen, and

[1] *G. Campbell Morgan: The Man and His Ministry* (Westwood, N. J.: Fleming H. Revell Company, 1930). Used by permission.

then did not preach again until two years had passed. At fifteen he began to preach quite often in country chapels and wherever the opportunity presented itself. About this time he completed his formal education, which was the equivalent of our American high-school graduation. His intense desire for knowledge inspired him to continue studying throughout his long and fruitful life, however, and he became one of the most respected Bible scholars of his time.

Significant in the early life of G. Campbell Morgan was a period of doubt which plagued him from the time he was nineteen until the age of twenty-one. John Harries quoted Morgan's own account of his experience:

> At the age of nineteen my early faith passed under eclipse, and I ceased to preach, which I had begun to do at the age of thirteen. For two years my Bible was shut; two years of sadness and sorrow. Strange, alluring, materialistic theories were in the air, and to these I turned. . . . In my despair I took all the books I had, placed them in a cupboard, turned the key, and there they remained for seven years. I bought a new Bible and began to read it with an open mind and a determined will. That Bible found me. The Book gave forth a glow which warmed my heart, and the Word of God which I read therein gave to my troubled soul the relief and satisfaction that I had sought for elsewhere. Since that time I have lived for one end—to preach the teachings of the Book that found me.[2]

From the time of this experience, G. Campbell Morgan was never the same. Small wonder one of his biographers made the title of the book of his life *The Man of the Word.* He was above all a preacher of the Word of God.

What was the secret of his success as a preacher and a pastor? He was often asked this question by young ministers, and he answered them, "Work, hard work, and again work." Until the last few months of his ministry Morgan was in his study without interruptions. He recommended to young preachers that they not look at the newspapers or read anything secular until after one o'clock in the afternoon, so that their minds could remain fresh while studying the Word.

[2] *Ibid.*

Characteristic of Dr. Morgan's method of sermon preparation was his habit of studying the Bible thoroughly before ever consulting a commentary. He wrote in his book *Preaching,* "For years I have made it a very careful and studied rule never to look at a commentary on a text, until I have spent time on the text alone." [3] He believed that the business of taking a text and looking to see all the other texts indicated in the references "is often destructive of real thinking and real Biblical work." He practiced the method of what he termed "firsthand thinking" on the scripture, rather than beginning the study by borrowing what other books have to say on the text.

Morgan's method has been used successfully by many noted preachers. Dr. Guthrie fastened his mind upon a text and then put on paper, just as they occurred to him, all the thoughts that seemed pertinent to the subject at hand. Archbishop Magee never looked about him for suggestions until he had first sketched his ideas as they came to him on the text. Alexander Maclaren thought about the text, without pencil or paper, until his thoughts began to clarify and develop. Charles E. Jefferson usually decided on his text and then "brooded" upon it for several days. All these men would agree with Morgan in recommending and practicing the method of studying the Word first, commentaries later.

Lest it be concluded that G. Campbell Morgan discounted completely the value of consulting many sources in the study of the Word, it must be emphasized that nothing could be further from the truth. On the contrary, few men have had a more complete, card-indexed, tabulated, catalogued file of information than Morgan. He was never at a loss as to where to find a reference or verify a quotation. He wasted very little time in searching for the data he needed.

It must be added that prayer played a most important role in his method of sermon preparation, although he did not agree with those who seemed to believe there is virtue in "long prayers." He once explained that he did not believe

[3] Used by permission of Fleming H. Revell Company.

in praying all night, because it might give the impression that he was trying to "force" God to act. He expresses his feelings thusly: "I can honestly say that I never have, and I never do settle down to a piece of work on my Bible without actual prayer for help." He goes on to say that he does not feel that "God needs a lot of hammering to persuade Him," and the actual prayer is relatively short.

G. Campbell Morgan believed preaching should contain three essentials: truth, clarity, and passion. His own preaching exemplified this ideal. He urged that preaching is not the proclamation of theory or the discussion of a doubt. "We are never preaching when we are hazarding speculations," he declared. "Neither is the declaration of negations preaching. Preaching is the proclamation of the Word, the truth as it has been revealed." He sees preaching as "the declaration of the grace of God to human need on the authority of the Throne of God; and it demands on the part of those who hear it that they show obedience to the thing declared." In G. Campbell Morgan's opinion, when a man preaches he stands squarely between human need and divine grace.

Morgan's preaching was a good example of what he would call analysis, synthesis, and application, the making of truth real to the needs of those who hear it. His own words show how he considered the right and wrong way to do this. He wrote, in *Preaching:*

> Here is an illustration of how not to do this. The text is, "God is a Spirit, and they that worship him must worship him in spirit and in truth." . . . Note the divisions made by a preacher who said, "First, we have presented to us the transcendental properties of the Divine nature. Secondly, we have the anthropomorphic relations under which those transcendental properties of the Divine nature stand revealed and become apprehensible." [4]

Need we go on? Morgan made such pedantic nonsense appear ridiculous as he declared that not one in a hundred would grasp these ideas when so presented.

[4] *Op. cit.*

He gives a better example, using the text, "Thy word have I hid in mine heart, that I might not sin against thee." Morgan suggests this type of treatment:

I. The Best Treasure—"Thy word"
II. The Best Place—"Hid in mine heart"
III. The Best Purpose—"That I might not sin against Thee" [5]

He believed in brief, clear introductions, and conclusions which "conclude, include, and preclude!" He saw the sermon as a "getting of the guns in position so that in the conclusion we can open fire on the enemy." He laments that too many preachers take so much time in getting the guns into position that they have to finish their sermons without firing a shot. Conclusions, to G. Campbell Morgan, were the "storming of the citadel of the will." The last sixty seconds of his sermons were dynamic moments in preaching.

Although most remembered for his biblical expositions and his great pastoral preaching, Dr. Morgan possessed the evangelistic zeal and fervor of a revivalist. He loved souls. His devotion to God and to the Word of God inspired him with the passion of a soul winner. His preaching went directly to the heart of the missionary, evangelistic, gospel message, namely, "Christ died for our sins."

A striking figure in his appearance, according to Harries, G. Campbell Morgan achieved a measure of his rapport by means of his physical qualities as well as his spiritual and mental powers. His keen, intellectual face, "a bright quick eye, which flashes with passion or wells with emotion; a resonant voice, which now blazons like a trumpet, then pleads in plaintive and irresistible pathos," made his delivery effective.

His gestures were numerous but never exaggerated, and they were always graceful and natural. His hands moved expressively, reminding the listener of what Quintilian said of their capabilities in expression:

[5] *Ibid.*

For other parts of the body assist the speaker, but these, I may say, speak themselves. By them we ask, we promise, we invoke, we dismiss, we threaten, we entreat, we deprecate, we express fear, joy, grief, our doubts, our assent, our penitence: we show moderation, or profusion; we mark number and time.[6]

"Truth, clarity, passion." G. Campbell Morgan loved the truth and found its precepts in the pages of the Book of books, the knowledge of which he made his chief intellectual goal. He sought and found the means to make the truth clear and present it simply and plainly, in the language of the people, so that even the unlearned and unwise need not "err therein." Passion, which is love on fire, burned within his soul and sent its warmth into the minds and hearts of those who heard him preach.

He preached the Word; he stirred human wills; he preached for a verdict. He exemplifies a worthy ideal of strong, vigorous, evangelical preaching.

[6] *Institutes of Oratory*, trans. H. E. Butler, Loeb Classical Library (Cambridge: Harvard University Press, 1921-1922), Bk. VII.

CHAPTER 24

John Henry Jowett

1864-1923

"With all my heart do I believe
that this gospel of redeeming grace
is the cardinal necessity of our time."

The words of John Henry Jowett, quoted by Arthur Porrit in his excellent biography of one of England's greatest pastors, contain the heart and soul of the energizing force that characterized the man and his message.[1] He was a preacher of the gospel of redeeming grace, and he preached like one who believed with all his heart that his message was the only hope of his time.

John Henry Jowett was born August 25, 1863, in Yorkshire, England, into the home of devoted and godly parents, whose lives provided the tremendous influence that helped to mold him into the man of God he became. He once said of his mother, whose two supreme interests seem to have been found in her home and in her church, that from her he gained his "sweetest inspirations." He is reported to have said, "Whenever I wish to think of a Christian man, I think of my father."

Jowett had planned to enter the practice of law, but he made his decision to preach after his Sunday-school teacher, J. W. Dewhirst, shocked him one day with the abrupt assertion, "I had always hoped that you would go into the ministry." The words stayed with him, and he realized that God was speaking to his heart by means of the saintly teacher. He described his experience thusly: "It was the result of no urgent argument, nor the issue of any calculation of profit and loss: it was shaped by a gracious constraint, and inclination born of love, a decision shaped by the worship of Jesus Christ."[2] He saw in his own case a genius which he

---

[1] *John Henry Jowett* (New York: George H. Doran Company, 1924).
[2] *Ibid.*, p. 40.

considered vital in the call of every minister, as he expressed it in his Lectures on Preaching to the students at Yale: "It is of momentous importance how a man enters the ministry. . . . He must be imperatively constrained by the eternal God." [3]

At the age of twenty-five, after completing his formal education at Edinburgh, he accepted the call to pastor the St. James Congregational Church in Newcastle on Tyne. Here Jowett's case was unique, since most young preachers begin their pastoral ministry in a small church and preach to larger congregations as they gain more experience. His first pastorate, however, was an influential church with a seating capacity of more than a thousand, and from the very first he preached to large crowds. Gerald Kennedy points out in *The Best of John Henry Jowett* that from his first Sunday until his last, as a pastor, "he never knew what it was like to preach to small crowds."

He remained as pastor here for seven years, during which time he met and married Lissie A. Winpenny. Upon the death of R. W. Dale in Carr's Lane, Birmingham, Jowett was called to fill this pulpit, which was one of the greatest Free Churches in England. It is believed by many that he reached his prime as he rose to the challenge of this pastorate. Elmer Homrighausen writes in *Great Pulpit Masters* that John Henry Jowett "reached the zenith of his pulpit power in Carr's Lane."

In 1911 Jowett accepted a call to the Fifth Avenue Presbyterian Church in New York City, and while there for seven fruitful years he preached in a sanctuary that was filled to capacity each Sunday, with many hundreds turned away unable to find seats in the church. He never did feel completely "at home" in New York, however, and in 1918 he returned to his beloved England to pastor at Westminster Chapel until his retirement a year before his death.

John Henry Jowett enjoyed preaching. His biographer describes the zeal and enthusiasm of his ministry: "All his

[3] John Henry Jowett, *The Preacher, His Life and Work* (New York: Eaton & Mains), p. 59. Copyright 1912, George H. Doran Company.

energies, spiritual, mental, nervous, and physical, were concentrated on preaching and preparation for preaching. He read, observed, thought, meditated, and brooded with a single eye to the pulpit; and he scorned delights and lived laborious days to perfect himself for his high calling." [4]

His own account of his study habits, in his book *The Preacher, His Life and Work* illustrates the intensity with which he viewed his task of preaching. He wrote:

> I used to hear the factory operatives passing my house on the way to the mills, where work began at six o'clock. I can recall the sound of their iron-clogs ringing through the street. The sound of the clogs fetched me out of bed and took me to my work. I can no longer hear the Yorkshire clogs, but I can see and hear my business-men as they start off early to earn their daily bread. And shall their minister be behind them in his quest of the Bread of Life? [5]

Jowett believed in preaching on great themes and mighty texts. He urged ministers to preach on the weighty texts "whose vastnesses almost terrify us as we approach them." His idea of great themes would include such as

> The holiness of God; the love of God; the grace of the Lord Jesus; the solemn wonders of the cross; the ministry of the Divine forgiveness; the fellowship of His sufferings; the power of the Resurrection; the blessedness of divine communion; the heavenly places in Christ Jesus; the mystical indwelling of the Holy Ghost; the abolition of the deadliness of death; the ageless life; our Father's house; the liberty and glory of the children of God. [6]

Gerald Kennedy expressed the heart of Jowett's preaching when he wrote: "If I were to describe the deepest impression Jowett's sermons have had on me, however, it would be his sense of the Gospel of Good News." [7] Indeed he did

---

[4] Elmer Homrighausen, *Great Pulpit Masters: John Henry Jowett.* (New York: Fleming H. Revell Co. n.d.), p. 257.
[5] *Op. cit.,* p. 116. Used by permission of Harper & Brothers.
[6] *Ibid.,* pp. 100-101.
[7] *The Best of John Henry Jowett* (New York: Harper & Brothers, 1948).

preach the good news—good news about God, about the Son of God, about the vanquishing of guilt and the forgiveness of sins. He preached the good news that Christ is master of the world, the flesh, and the devil. It is good news, as Porrit put it, "about the transfiguration of sorrow and the withering of a thousand bitter roots of anxiety and care. It is to be good news about the stingless death and the spoiled and beaten grave."

When Jowett preached, the "whole man preached." People who heard him said his voice preached, and so did "his hands, his lips, his face, his gestures, his life!" He read his sermons from a manuscript, but his words were so meaningful and his spirit so fervent that little if any of the impact of his message was lost through this method of delivery. Homrighausen, writing of his style, declared: "One gets the impression that he wrestled with the English language to make it subservient to the message he had experienced in his own soul." His hobby seemed to be the study of words, and he always seemed to be able to find the exact word which made his carefully chosen sentences an example of artistry in English prose.

Jowett's source book was the Bible. The scripture with him was not seen as a springboard from which to leap out in any direction which a preacher's mind may send him, but a form for the very body and soul of his sermon. He was never far away from the biblical word. He decried topical preaching. Much of his preaching was expository in nature, and all of it was biblical. In addition to the Bible as his first source, *Pilgrim's Progress* was a second and frequent source book for Jowett's sermon material. When speaking of a human experience, he almost always quoted Bunyan's story of what Christian did under similar circumstances on his journey to the Celestial City.

Jowett used very little humor in the pulpit, and that which was employed was in good taste, serving a purpose, never for its own sake or as an end in itself. He quoted poetry frequently—usually at least once or twice in each sermon—and his illustrations were varied and meaningful.

Illustrations were somewhat lengthy in Jowett's sermons, but they always made the point clear.

A glance at some of his sermon titles or some of the titles of his books reveals something of the heart and soul of John Henry Jowett's preaching. "God, Our Contemporary" makes us want to hear more of what the preacher has to say in this message. "The Transfigured Church" is a portrayal of the possibilities within the church, and offers a striking topic for a preacher's theme. "The High Calling" is the title given to Jowett's meditations on Paul's letter to the Philippians, and "The Silver Lining" is the title of his message of hope and cheer for the troubled and tried.

One observer saw running through all the preaching of this man "an emphasis on the gospel as comfort." Jowett often quoted Dr. Parker's words, "Preach to broken hearts." In his lectures he is quoted as pleading: "One thing is perfectly clear, the merely dictatorial will never heal the broken in heart, or bind up their bleeding wounds. . . . The gospel of a broken heart demands the ministry of bleeding hearts. As soon as we have ceased to bleed, we have ceased to bless." [8]

John Henry Jowett never ceased to "bleed." With bleeding heart he preached comfort to the afflicted, redemption to the lost, forgiveness to the guilty, communion to the lonely, and the indwelling of the Holy Ghost to the believer. His was the ministry of a bleeding heart, and his is a worthy ideal in evangelical preaching.

[8] Jowett, *The Preacher, His Life & Work*, p. 108.

SUGGESTED READINGS

Many of the books listed below are now out of print but are still valuable where available.

CHAPTER 1 (Wycliffe)

Cadman, Samuel Parkes. *The Three Religious Leaders of Oxford.* New York: The Macmillan Company, 1916.

Cameron, Allan. *Great Men and Movements of the Christian Church.* Paisley: Alexander Gardner, 1914.

Lechler, Gotthard V. *John Wycliff and His English Precursors.* London: The Religious Tract Society, 1884.

MacIntosh, J. S. *The Breakers of the Yoke.* Philadelphia: Press of Henry B. Ashmead, 1884.

McFarlane, Kenneth Bruce. *John Wycliffe and the Beginnings of English Nonconformity.* New York: The Macmillan Company, 1952.

Workman, Herbert Brook. *The Dawn of the Reformation.* London: C. H. Kelly, 1901-2.

——. *Writings of John Wycliffe.* London: Religion Tract Society, n.d.

CHAPTER 2 (Huss)

Cameron, Allan. *Op. cit.*

Gillett, Ezra Hall. *The Life and Times of John Huss.* New York: Sheldon and Company, 1863.

Huss, John. *The Letters of John Huss.* London: Hodder and Stoughton, Ltd., 1904.

Kuhns, Levi Oscar. *John Huss: The Witness.* New York: Eaton and Mains, 1907.

Roubiczek, Paul. *Warrior of God.* London: Nicholson and Watson, 1947.

Sample, Robert F. *Beacon Lights of the Reformation.* Philadelphia: Presbyterian Board of Publication & Sabbath School Work, 1880.

Schaff, Phillip. *The New Schaff-Herzog Encyclopedia.* Ed. Lefferts A. Loetscher. Grand Rapids Mich.: Baker Book House, 1955.

Workman, Herbert Brook. *Op. cit.*

CHAPTER 3 (Luther)

Bainton, Roland H. *Here I Stand.* Nashville: Abingdon Press, 1950.
Bayne, Peter. *Martin Luther, His Life and Work.* London: Cassell and Co., Ltd., 1887.
Boehmer, Heinrich. *Luther in the Light of Recent Research.* New York: The Christian Herald, 1916.
Booth, Edwin P. *Martin Luther, Oak of Saxony.* New York: Round Table Press, 1933.
Boyer, Merle W. *Luther in Protestantism Today.* New York: Association Press, 1958.
Cameron, Allan. *Op. cit.*
Fife, Robert H. *The Revolt of Martin Luther.* New York: Columbia University Press, 1957.
Lindemann, Henry. *Martin Luther, Man of God.* New York: The Exposition Press, 1955.
Luther, Martin. *Reformation Writings.* Tr. Bertram E. Woolf. New York: Philosophical Library, 1953.
————. *Works.* St. Louis, Mo.: Concordia Publishing House, 1956-58; Philadelphia: Muhlenberg Press.
Nuelson, John Louis. *Luther, the Leader.* New York: Eaton and Mains, 1906.
————. *Letters of Spiritual Counsel.* Ed. Theodore G. Tappert. Philadelphia: The Westminster Press, 1955.
Plass, E. W. *This Is Luther.* St. Louis: Concordia Publishing House, 1948.

CHAPTER 4 (Zwingli)

Cameron, Allan. *Op. cit.*
Davies, Rupert Eric. *The Problem of Authority in the Continental Reformers.* London: The Epworth Press, 1946.
MacIntosh, J. S. *Op. cit.*
Schaff, Phillip. *Op. cit.*
Sample, Robert F. *Op. cit.*
Simpson, Samuel. *The Life of Ulrich Zwingli.* New York: The Baker and Taylor Company, 1902.
Zwingli, Ulrich. *Zwingli and Bullinger.* Selected tr. G. W. Bromley. Philadelphia: The Westminster Press, 1953.

CHAPTER 5 (Melanchthon)

Cameron, Allan. *Op. cit.*
Hildebrandt, Franz. *Melanchthon: Alien or Ally?* Cambridge, England: Cambridge University Press, 1946.
Manschreck, Clyde L. *Melanchthon, The Quiet Reformer.* Nashville: Abingdon Press, 1958.

Melanchthon, Philip. *The Loci Communes of Philip Melanchthon.* Tr. Charles L. Hill. Boston: Meador Publishing Company, 1944.

Richard, J. W. *Philip Melanchthon: The Preceptor of Germany.* New York: G. P. Putnam's Sons, 1898.

Schaff, Philip. *St. Augustine, Melanchthon, Neander.* London: James Nisbet & Company, 1886.

CHAPTER 6 (Knox)

Cameron, Allan. *Op. cit.*

Crook, Isaac. *John Knox, The Reformer.* New York: Eaton and Maines, 1906.

Dickenson, William Croft. (Ed.). *John Knox's History of the Reformation in Scotland.* New York: Philosophical Library, Inc., 1950.

Kleiser, Grenville. *The World's Great Sermons.* New York: Funk & Wagnalls Company, 1908.

Knox, John. *Works.* Ed. David Laing. Edinburgh: Wodrow Society, 1848.

MacGregor, Geddes. *The Thundering Scot.* Philadelphia: The Westminster Press, 1957.

MacIntosh, J. S. *Op. cit.*

McCrie, Thomas. *The Life of John Knox.* London: H. G. Bohn, 1854.

Pond, Enoch. *Memoirs of John Knox.* Boston: Sabbath School Society, 1855.

CHAPTER 7 (Calvin)

Beza, Theodore. *The Life of John Calvin.* Philadelphia: J. Whetham, 1836.

Calvin, John. *The Deity of Christ and Other Sermons.* Tr. Leroy Nixon. Grand Rapids, Mich.: William B. Eerdmans Publishing Company, 1950.

————. *The Mystery of Godliness and Other Selected Sermons.* Grand Rapids, Mich.: William B. Eerdmans Publishing Company, 1950.

Cameron, Allan. *Op. cit.*

Davies, Alfred Thomas. *John Calvin.* London: H. E. Walter, 1946.

————. *John Calvin, Many-Sided Genius.* New York: American Track Society, 1947.

Harkness, Georgia. *John Calvin: The Man and His Ethics.* Nashville: Abingdon Press, 1958.

Henry, Paul Emil. *The Life and Times of John Calvin.* New York: R. Carter & Brother, 1851-52.

Hyma, Albert. *The Life of John Calvin.* Grand Rapids, Mich.: William B. Eerdmans Publishing Company, 1943.

Nixon, Leroy. *John Calvin: Expository Preacher*. Grand Rapids, Mich.: William B. Eerdmans Publishing Company, 1950.
Parker, Thomas H. L. *The Oracles of God*. London: Lutterworth Press, 1947.
Walker, Williston. *John Calvin*. New York: G. P. Ptunam's Sons, 1906.

CHAPTER 8 (Edwards)

Blackwood, Andrew W. *The Protestant Pulpit*. Nashville: Abingdon Press. 1947.
Edwards, Jonathan. *Edwards on Revivals*. New York: Dunning and Spalding, 1832.
———. *Freedom of the Will*. Ed. Paul Ramsey. New Haven, Conn.: Yale University Press, 1957. (This volume is one of a series, *Works of Jonathan Edwards*, ed. Perry Miller.)
———. *The Philosophy of Jonathan Edwards*. Ed. Harvey G. Townsend. Eugene, Ore.: University of Oregon Press, 1955.
———. *Puritan Sage*. Ed. Vergilius Ferm. New York: Library Publishers, 1953.
———. *The Works of Prendent-Edwards*. 4 vols. New York: Leavitt and Allen, 1851-52.
Fish, Henry C. *Pulpit Eloquence*. New York: Dodd, Mead & Company, 1856.
Gerstner, John H. *Steps to Salvation*. Philadelphia: The Westminster Press, 1960.
McGiffert, Arthur C. *Jonathan Edwards*. New York: Harper & Brothers, 1932.
Miller, Perry. *Jonathan Edwards*. New York: William Sloan Associates, 1949.
Turnbull, Ralph G. *Jonathan Edwards, The Preacher*. Grand Rapids, Mich.: Baker Book House, 1958.
Winslow, Ola Elizabeth. *Jonathan Edwards*. New York: The Macmillan Company, 1940.
Turnbull, Ralph G. *Jonathan Edwards, the Preacher*. Grand Rapids, Mich.: Baker Book House, 1958.
Winslow, Ola Elizabeth. *Jonathan Edwards*. New York: The Macmillan Company, 1940.

CHAPTER 9 (Wesley)

Burtner, Robert W., and Chiles, Robert E. *A Compend of Wesley's Theology*. Nashville: Abingdon Press, 1954.
Cadman, Samuel Parkes. *Op. cit.*
Cameron, Richard M. *The Rise of Methodism*. New York: Philosophical Library, 1954.

Cannon, William R. *The Theology of John Wesley.* Nashville: Abingdon Press, 1946.

Church, Leslie F. *Knight of the Burning Heart.* Nashville: Abingdon Press, 1938.

Doughty, W. L. *John Wesley, The Preacher.* London: The Epworth Press, 1955.

Edwards, Maldwyn. *John Wesley and the Eighteenth Century.* Nashville: Abingdon Press, 1933.

Gill, Frederick C. *John Wesley's Prayers.* Nashville: Abingdon Press, 1951.

————. *Through the Year with John Wesley.* London: The Epworth Press, 1954.

Hildebrandt, Franz. *Christianity According to the Wesleys.* London: The Epworth Press, 1956.

Lee, Umphrey. *The Lord's Horseman.* Nashville: Abingdon Press, 1954.

Lindstrom, Harold G. A. *Wesley and Sanctification.* London: The Epworth Press, n. d.

Luccock, Halford E., Hutchinson, Paul, and Goodloe, Robert W. *The Story of Methodism.* Nashville: Abingdon Press, 1949.

McConnell, Francis J. *Evangelicals, Revolutionists, and Idealists.* Nashville: Abingdon-Cokesbury Press, 1942.

————. *John Wesley.* Nashville: Abingdon Press, 1939.

McNeer, May, and Ward, Lynd. *John Wesley.* Nashville: Abingdon Press, 1951.

Piette, Maximin. *John Wesley in the Evolution of Protestantism.* New York: Sheed and Ward, Inc., 1937.

Vulliamy, C. E. *John Wesley.* London: The Epworth Press, 1954.

Wesley, John. *The Journal of John Wesley.* 2 vols. New York: Eaton & Mains, 1904.

————. *The Letters of John Wesley.* 8 vols. London: The Epworth Press, 1931.

————. *Christian Perfection.* Cincinnati: Poe & Hitchcock, 1865.

————. *Forty-four Sermons.*

————. *Explanatory Notes Upon the New Testament.* New York: Eaton & Mains, 1900.

————. *Wesley's Standard Sermons,* ed. E. H. Sugden. London: The Epworth Press, 1956.

————. *The Works of John Wesley.* 14 vols. Grand Rapids, Mich.: Zondervan Publishing House, 1958.

Whiteley, J. H. *Wesley's England.* Naperville, Ill.: Alec R. Allenson, Inc., 1954.

CHAPTER 10 (Whitefield)

Belcher, Joseph. *George Whitefield: A Biography.* New York: American Tract Society, 1857.

Beldon, Albert David. *George Whitefield. The Awakener.* London: S. Low, Marston & Company, 1930.

Billingsley, Amos Stevens, *The Life of George Whitefield.* New York: John B. Alden, 1889.

Butler, Dugald. *John Wesley and George Whitefield in Scotland.* Edinburgh: W. Blackwood & Sons, 1898.

Gillies, John. *Memoirs of the Life of Reverend George Whitefield.* Hartford, Conn.: Edwin Hunt, 1847.

Hardy, Edwin N. *George Whitefield, the Matchless Soul Winner.* New York: American Tract Society, 1938.

Henry, Stuart Clark. *George Whitefield: Wayfaring Witness.* Nashville: Abingdon Press, 1957.

Macartney, Clarence E. *Six Kings of the American Pulpit.* Philadelphia: Westminster Press, 1942.

McLeister, Clara. *Men and Women of Deep Piety.* Cincinnati: God's Revivalist Press, 1920.

Ninde, Edward S. *George Whitefield, Prophet—Preacher.* New York: Abingdon Press, 1924.

Whitefield, George. *Sermon Outlines.* Ed. Sheldon B. Quincer. Grand Rapids, Mich.: William B. Eerdmans Publishing Company, 1956.

CHAPTER 11 (Fletcher)

Benson, Joseph. *The Life of the Rev. John W. De La Flechere.* New York: The Methodist Book Concern, 1914.

Brooks, Phillips. *Lectures on Preaching.* New York: E. P. Dutton & Company, 1877.

Cameron, Richard M. *Op. cit.*

Fletcher, John W. *The Works of the Reverend John Fletcher.* London: John Mason, 1859-60.

Luccock, Halford. *In The Minister's Workshop.* Nashville: Abingdon Press, 1944.

Luccock, Halford, *et. al. Op. cit.*

Sangster, W. E. *The Craft of Sermon Construction.* Philadelphia: The Westminster Press, 1951.

CHAPTER 12 (Asbury)

Asbury, Francis. *The Heart of Asbury's Journal.* Ed. Ezra S. Tipple. New York: Eaton and Maines, 1904.

Asbury, Herbert. *A Methodist Saint.* New York: Alfred A. Knopf, Inc., 1927.

Cameron, Richard M. *Op. cit.*

Clark, Elmer T., Potts, J. Manning, and Payton, Jacob S. (eds.).

The Journal and Letters of Francis Asbury. 3 vols. Nashville: Abingdon Press, 1958.

DuBose, Horace M. *Francis Asbury.* Nashville: Smith and Lamar, 1916.

Duren, William L. *Francis Asbury.* New York: The Macmillan Company, 1928.

Feeman, Harlan L. *Francis Asbury's Silver Trumpet.* Nashville: Privately printed, 1950.

Mains, George P. *Francis Asbury.* New York: Eaton & Mains, 1909.

Tipple, Ezra S. *Francis Asbury, The Prophet of the Long Road.* New York: Methodist Book Concern, 1916.

CHAPTER 13 (Simeon)

Moule, Handley C. G. *Charles Simeon.* London: Methuen and Company, 1914.

Simeon, Charles. *Expository Outlines on the Whole Bible.* 21 vols. Grand Rapids, Mich.: Zondervan Publishing House, 1955-56.

Warren, Max A. C. *Charles Simeon.* London: Church Book Room Press, 1947.

Wesley, John. *The Journal of John Wesley. Op. cit.*

CHAPTER 14 (Cartwright)

Cameron, Richard M. *Op. cit.*

Cartwright, Peter. *Autobiography of Peter Cartwright.* Ed. W. P. Strickland. New York: Carlton & Porter, 1857.

———. *Autobiography.* Ed. Charles L. Wallis. Nashville: Abingdon Press, 1956.

Greenbie, Sydney. *Hoofbeats to Heaven.* Penobscot, Me.: Traversity Press, 1955.

Lawson, James G. *Deeper Experiences of Famous Christians.* Fort Wayne, Ind.: Glad Tidings Publishing Company, 1911.

Luccock, Halford, *et. al. Op. cit.*

Macartney, Clarence E. *Sons of Thunder, Pulpit Powers of the Past.* New York: Fleming H. Revell Company, 1929.

Sweet, William Warren. *Revivalism In America.* New York: Charles Scribner's Sons, 1944.

CHAPTER 15 (Finney)

Beardsley, Frank G. *A Mighty Winner of Souls.* New York: American Tract Society, 1937.

Edman, Victor Raymond. *Finney Lives On.* Westwood, N. J.: Fleming H. Revell Company, 1951.

Finney, Charles G. *Charles G. Finney, An Autobiography.* London: Hodder & Stoughton, Ltd., 1882.

———. *Lectures on Revivals.* Oberlin, Ohio: E. J. Goodrich, 1868.

———. *Memoirs*. New York: A. S. Barnes & Company, 1876.
———. *Sermons on Gospel Themes*. Westwood, N. J.; Fleming H. Revell Company, 1876.
Harding, William Henry. *Finney's Life and Lectures*. Grand Rapids, Mich.: Zondervan Publishing Company, 1943.
Hills, Aaron M. *Life of Charles G. Finney*. Cincinnati: Office of God's Revivalist. 1902.
Miller, Basil W. *Charles G. Finney: He Prayed Down Revivals*. Grand Rapids, Mich.: Zondervan Publishing Company, 1941.
Sweet, William Warren. *Op. cit.*

CHAPTER 16 (Beecher)

Abbott, Lyman. *Henry Ward Beecher*. Boston: Houghton Mifflin Company, 1903.
Beecher, Henry Ward. *Lecture-Room Talks*. Ed. T. S. Ellinwood. New York: J. B. Ford & Company, 1872.
———. Plymouth Pulpit. 10 vols. New York: Fords, Howard, and Hulbert, 1869-84.
———. *Yale Lectures on Preaching*. Boston: Pilgrim Press, 1902.
Beecher, William C. *A Biography of Reverend Henry Ward Beecher*. New York: C. L. Webster Company, 1888.
Brastow, Lewis O. *Representative Modern Preachers*. New York: The Macmillan Company, 1904.
Hibben, Paxton. *Henry Ward Beecher: An American Portrait*. New York: The Press of The Reader's Club, 1942.
Howard, Joseph. *Life of Henry Ward Beecher*. Philadelphia: Hubbard Brother, 1887.
Macartney, Clarence E. *Op. cit.*

CHAPTER 17 (Robertson)

Blackwood, James Russell. *The Soul of Frederick W. Robertson*. New York: Harper & Brothers, 1947.
Brastow, Lewis O. *Op. cit.*
Robertson, Frederick W. *Expository Lectures on Corinthians*. London: K. Paul, Trench, Trubner, & Company, 1902.
———. *The Human Race and Other Sermons*. New York: Harper & Brothers, 1881.
———. *Life, Letters, Lectures, and Addresses of Frederick W. Robertson*. Ed. S. A. Brooke. New York: Harper & Brothers, 1903.
———. *Sermons on Christian Doctrine*. New York: E. P. Dutton & Company, 1906.
———. *Sermons Preached at Brighton*. New York: E. P. Dutton & Company, 1904.

————. *Sermons Preached at Trinity Chapel.* Boston: Tickner & Fields, 1858.

CHAPTER 18 (Maclaren)

Maclaren, Alexander. *Expositions of the Holy Scriptures.* 17 vols. Grand Rapids, Mich.: William B. Eerdmans Publishing Company, 1944.

————. *Our Father.* Grand Rapids, Mich.: William B. Eerdmans Publishing Company, 1946.

————. *The Secret of Power and Other Sermons.* New York: Funk & Wagnalls Company, 1905.

————. *Sermon Outlines.* Ed. Sheldon B. Quincer. Grand Rapids, Mich.: William B. Eerdmans Publishing Company, 1954.

————. *Sermons Preached in Manchester.* London: Macmillan and Company, 1881.

Maclaren, E. T. *Dr. Maclaren of Manchester.* New York: The Macmillan Company, 1911.

CHAPTER 19 (Spurgeon)

Brastow, Lewis O. *Op. cit.*

Conwell, Russell H. *Life of Charles Haddon Spurgeon.* Philadelphia: Edgewood Publishing Company, 1897.

Cook, Richard B. *The Wit and Wisdom of Reverend Charles Haddon Spurgeon.* Lenox Publishing Company, 1892.

Day, Richard E. *The Shadow of the Broad Brim.* Philadelphia: The Judson Press, 1934.

Ellis, James J. *Charles Haddon Spurgeon.* London: J. Nisbet & Company, 1891.

Great Pulpit Masters. Westwood, N. J.: Fleming H. Revell Company, 1949-51). Vol. 2.

Pike, Godfrey H. *Charles Haddon Suprgeon.* New York: Funk & Wagnalls Company, 1892.

Shindler, Robert. *From the Usher's Desk to the Tabernacle Pulpit.* New York: A. C. Armstrong. 1892.

Spurgeon, Charles Haddon. *C. H. Spurgeon's Autobiography.* Ed. D. O. Fuller. Grand Rapids, Mich.: Zondervan Publishing Company, 1946.

————. *Charles Haddon Spurgeon: A Biographical Sketch.* London: A. Melrose, 1903.

————. *Sermons.* Grand Rapids, Mich.: Zondervan Publishing Company, 1952.

————. *My Sermon Notes.* Westwood, N. J.: Fleming H. Revell Company, 1956.

————. *Spurgeon's Expository Encyclopedia.* 15 vols. Grand Rapids, Mich.: Baker Book House, 1951-52.

————. *Spurgeon's Lectures to His Students*. Ed. D. O. Fuller. Grand Rapids. Mich.: Zondervan Publishing Company, 1945.

CHAPTER 20 (Brooks)

Addison, Daniel D. *The Clergy in American Life and Letters*. New York: The Macmillan Company, 1900.
Allen, Alexander V. G. *Life and Letters of Phillips Brooks*. New York: E. P. Dutton & Company, 1900.
Brastow, Lewis O. *Op. cit.*
Brooks, Phillips. *The Candle of the Lord*. New York: E. P. Dutton & Company, 1903.
————. *The Excellence of Our Calling*. Abridged by Thomas F. Chilcote, Jr. New York: E. P. Dutton & Company, 1954.
————. *Lectures on Preaching*. New York: E. P. Dutton & Company, 1877.
————. *The Light of the World*. New York: E. P. Dutton & Company, 1902.
————. *Selected Sermons*. Ed. William Scarlett. New York: E. P. Dutton & Company, 1949.
————. *Sermons Preached in English Churches*. New York: E. P. Dutton & Company, 1901.
Donald, E. W. *Sermons of the Clergy of Trinity Church*. Cambridge: The Riverside Press, 1893.
Lawrence, William. *The Life of Phillips Brooks*. New York: Harper & Brothers, 1930.
Macartney, Clarence E. *Op. cit.*

CHAPTER 21 (Moody)

Albus, Harry James. *The Boy From Northfield*. Grand Rapids, Mich.: William B. Eerdmans Publishing Company, 1949.
Bradford, Gamaliel. *D. L. Moody, A Worker in Souls*. New York: George H. Doran Company, 1927.
Fitt, Arthur Percy. *Moody Still Lives*. Westwood, N. J.: Fleming H. Revell, Company, 1936.
Great Pulpit Masters. Op. cit.
Hanson, John Wesley. *The Life and Works of Dwight L. Moody*. Chicago: W. B. Conkey, 1900.
Moody, Dwight L. *Fifty Sermons of Dwight L. Moody*. Cleveland: J. B. Savage, n. d.
————. *The New Sermons of Dwight L. Moody*. New York: Harry S. Goodspeed, 1880.
————. *A Treasury of Dwight L. Moody*. Ed. Harry J. Albus. Grand Rapids, Mich.: William B. Eerdmans Publishing Company, 1949.
Moody, William R., *The Life of Dwight L. Moody*. New York:

Fleming H. Revell Company, 1900.
Smith, Wilbur M. *An Annotated Bibliography of D. L. Moody.* Chicago: Moody Press, 1948.
Torrey, R. A. *Why God Used D. L. Moody.* Westwood, N. J.: Fleming H. Revell Company, 1923.
Wilson, Philip Whitwell. *The Meaning of Moody.* Westwood, N. J.: Fleming H. Revell Company, 1938.

CHAPTER 22 (Meyer)

Fullerton, William Young. *F. B. Meyer, A Biography.* London: Marshall, Morgan & Scott, Ltd., n. d.
Great Pulpit Masters. Op. cit.
Mann, A. Chester. *F. B. Meyer.* Westwood, N. J.: Fleming H. Revell Company, 1929.
Meyer, Frederick Brotherton. *Hints for Lay Preachers.* Westwood, N. J.: Fleming H. Revell Company, n. d.
———. *Paul, A Servant of Jesus Christ.* Westwood, N. J.: Fleming H. Revell Company, 1897.
———. *Peter: Fisherman, Disciple, Apostle.* Westwood, N. J.: Fleming H. Revell Company, 1920.
———. *The Way Into The Holiest.* Westwood, N. J.: Fleming H. Revell Company, 1893.
———. *Expository Preaching: Plans and Methods.* Garden City, N. Y.: George H. Doran Company, 1912.
Sinclair, Hugh. *Voices of Today.* London: James Clark & Company, 1912.

CHAPTER 23 (Morgan)

Harries, John. *G. Campbell Morgan: The Man and His Ministry.* Westwood, N. J.: Fleming H. Revell Company, 1930.
Morgan, G. Campbell. *Christian Principles.* Westwood, N. J.: Fleming H. Revell Company, 1908.
———. *The Crises of the Christ.* Westwood, N. J.: Fleming H. Revell Company, 1903.
———. *Evangelism.* Westwood, N. J.: Fleming H. Revell Company, 1904.
———. *Great Chapters of the Bible.* London: The Book Room of Westminster Congregational Church, 1935.
———. *The Great Physician.* Westwood, N. J.: Fleming H. Revell Company, 1937.
———. *The Parables and Metaphors of Our Lord.* Westwood, N. J.: Fleming H. Revell Company, 1943.
———. *Preaching.* Westwood, N. J.: Fleming H. Revell Company, 1937.

————. *This Was His Faith.* Ed. Jill Morgan. Westwood, N. J.: Fleming H. Revell Company, 1952.

————. *The Triumphs of Faith.* Westwood, N. J.: Fleming H. Revell Company, 1944.

————. *The Westminster Pulpit; The Preaching of G. Campbell Morgan.* 10 vols. Westwood, N. J.: Fleming H. Revell Company, 1954-55.

Morgan, Jill. *A Man of The Word; Life of G. Campbell Morgan.* Westwood, N. J.: Fleming H. Revell Company, 1951.

CHAPTER 24 (Jowett)

Great Pulpit Masters. Op. cit.

Jowett, John Henry. *Apostolic Optimism.* New York: George H. Doran Company, 1914.

————. *The Best of John Henry Jowett.* Ed. Gerald Kennedy. New York: Harper & Brothers, 1948.

————. *God, Our Contemporary.* Westwood, N. J.: Fleming H. Revell Company, 1922.

————. *Life in the Heights.* New York: George H. Doran. 1925.

————. *The Passion for Souls.* New York: Grossett & Dunlap, Inc., 1942.

————. *The Preacher, His Life and Work.* New York: Eaton and Mains. Copyright George H. Doran Co. 1912.

————. *The Whole Armour of God.* Westwood, N. J.: Fleming H. Revell Company, 1916.

Porritt, Arthur. *John Henry Jowett.* New York: George H. Doran Company, 1924.

INDEX